"With [...] only offers a theological [...] provides a path to
Resurr[...] [...]k is a reminder of
why theology matters and how a little scholarship goes a
long way."
—**Rev. Stephen Cady**, Senior Minister, Asbury First United
Methodist Church, Rochester, NY

"In his deeply personal voice, J. J. Warren courageously
calls the United Methodist Church to examine again the
distinction between what is often assumed to be its tradition and the deep roots of tradition that have long
embraced an inclusive worldview."
—**Thomas V. Wolfe**, President and CEO, Iliff School of
Theology

"*Reclaiming Church* is insightful, informative and inspi-
rational. This fresh and personal look at human sexuality
and the role of the Church is a must-read and a tremen-
dous opportunity to have a deeper and new conversation
with those you may agree with or disagree with concerning
human sexuality."
—**Olu Brown**, Lead Pastor, Impact Church

"J. J. Warren is no flash in the pan. I, along with many
others, first encountered J. J.'s powerful voice as I watched
a livestream of his impassioned speech on the floor of the
2019 Special Session of the UMC General Conference.
Now, in this book, J. J. demonstrates that his speech flowed
from a deep well of theological and practical thinking

about the nature and mission of the church. J. J. offers a beautiful vision of a truly inclusive church and a clear road map of how those whom the church has marginalized can reclaim their rightful place at the center of the church's identity and work."
—**Theodore Hickman-Maynard,** Associate Dean for Students and Community Life and Assistant Professor of Black Church Studies, Boston University School of Theology

"For people who are passionate about reforming their denomination, J. J. is someone you should listen to. Through passionate storytelling and very accessible theological concepts, he walks readers of all backgrounds toward an idea of Church that not only is appealing but also gives me hope that perhaps that we, the Church, can evolve into the people we always were meant to be. *Reclaiming Church* gives us a picture of a better church for all of us, straight folks included."
—**Kevin Garcia,** queer public theologian, digital pastor, and intuitive soul coach

Reclaiming Church

A Call to Action for
RELIGIOUS REJECTS

J. J. Warren

ABINGDON PRESS / NASHVILLE

RECLAIMING CHURCH
A CALL TO ACTION FOR RELIGIOUS REJECTS

Copyright © 2020 Abingdon Press

Library of Congress Control Number: 2019954213

ISBN 13: 978-1-5018-9606-4

20 21 22 23 24 25 26 27 28 29 — 10 9 8 7 6 5 4 3 2 1
MANUFACTURED IN THE UNITED STATES OF AMERICA

CONTENTS

FOREWORD

You have to give them hope.

—Harvey Milk

As a young person, I always knew there was something different about me, although I didn't have a name for it. As friends began dating, I found myself feeling increasingly unlike them. I had no interest at all in having a boyfriend. I didn't want to go to the homecoming or the prom. What was wrong with me? I felt increasingly alienated from so many of my peers. Their lives seemed foreign to me. As much as I tried to join in activities that centered on creating romantic ties with the opposite sex, it always felt like something wasn't right.

The one place that made me feel like I had a home was my local church. Our youth group was a sanctuary for so many of us. We were invited to be our authentic selves (even when we weren't sure what that meant) and encouraged to become leaders. We came from several different high schools where, for the most part, we didn't quite fit in. Years later, at a beach where we had shared so many memories, we gathered for a youth group reunion. One of my friends said, "Thank God for our youth group—it was the one place we misfits found a place to belong."

It would not be until my first year of seminary that I realized there was a name for what I was feeling and for who I was. At seminary, I listened to the stories of my gay and lesbian classmates and realized their stories sounded a lot like mine. When I was finally able to say to myself, "I am a lesbian," all the confusing pieces of my life came together, and I experienced a profound sense of wholeness and peace.

Looking back, I wish I could talk to my younger self, look her in the eyes and tell her, "You're going to be OK. You are going to figure out what is different about you, and it will be a great gift. It will deepen your empathy with those who are different. It will bring you a powerful community. And you will find deep and abiding love." What a difference that hopeful conversation would have made in my journey!

If you are wondering if there is a place for you, if you wonder if you will ever find community, if you are feeling like a reject because of what others say about you (or what you might think about yourself), this book is for you. It will give you hope when hope feels lost.

And it has its origins in a most hopeless event:

The General Conference of The United Methodist Church, held every four years, is the best and worst of times. United Methodist delegates, bishops, general church staff, and observers gather from around the world to determine who we will be for the next four years, revising our ways to meet the changing needs of the church to respond in ministry to a changing world. This gathering is accompanied by spirited worship, moving sermons, and powerful testimony of the ways United Methodists are sharing the love of God with neighbors around the world. It is also a time of political maneuvering, jockeying for power, and raucous debates that at times debase the diversity reflected in God's beloved children.

It was the latter description that filled the convention center in St. Louis on February 23-26, 2019, for the Special Session of the General Conference. The church had reached a breaking point regarding an understanding of the role of queer United Methodists in the life and ministry of the denomination. In response to the tension, a Commission on a Way Forward was convened with the purpose of proposing a way to strengthen church unity and mission while acknowledging the different opinions regarding homosexuality held by faithful United Methodists.

The Commission worked for more than two years perfecting the One Church Plan, which removed anti-queer language from the *Book of Discipline* (BOD) while acknowledging that different contexts and personal conscience would reflect different responses to the role of queer people in the church. This plan was accepted by a large majority of the Council of Bishops. The delegates, however, rejected the plan and opted instead to focus their work on the Traditional Plan, which not only continued the anti-queer language of the BOD but doubled down on enforcement and punishment.

By February 25, it was clear where the votes were heading, and despair hung over the dais where I sat with my fellow bishops. One bishop was so agitated that he couldn't sit in his chair but kept pacing back and forth behind us, muttering, "They are destroying our church." Some bishops were in tears. Others put their heads down in prayer. A thick pall had fallen over the convention center.

And then, a young person from Upper New York was called to the microphone. Within three minutes, J. J. Warren had dispelled the gloom. It felt like Pentecost, as the Holy Spirit breathed life into the somber hall and people were brought to their feet with shouts of "Amen!" and applause.

J. J. had helped us remember what we all were forgetting: that the purpose of the church is to offer Jesus.

And J. J. has continued to help us remember.

General Conference delegates did indeed vote to adopt the Traditional Plan—one that had, at multiple times, been deemed unconstitutional by the Judicial Council (the "Supreme Court" of the denomination)—and tightened restrictions against queer United Methodists and those who would offer them the full ministry of the church. The vote perhaps dealt a mortal blow to the denomination itself and once again wounded its queer members and our loved ones. The news of the delegates' vote reverberated around the world, as news outlets reported the impact of the vote on local communities. Clergy wondered how they could continue to serve in such a church. Lay members were embarrassed by the General Conference actions taken. (One woman in my conference told me how she turned her United Methodist canvas bags inside out when she shopped, so no one would see what she was carrying. She was, for the first time in her life, embarrassed to be a United Methodist.) And queer people were once again left bloodied by a vote about them.

J. J.'s speech and the hope he inspired at General Conference sent him on a cross-country trek, a one-man evangelistic mission, to remind the church to give folks Jesus. All the folks, not some of the folks. And especially, to queer people, J. J. has offered with his book and his mission the gift of hope: hope that Scripture really is liberating; hope that God's love is for all with no exceptions; hope in Jesus, who breaks open new life for everyone; hope in the Holy Spirit, who is forever expanding the circle of who is included; and hope in a community made richer by diversity.

May the hope found in this book be a healing balm for those wounded by the actions of General Conference. May it offer a hope in the face of bullying and belittling. May it be a wake-up call to those who have grown complacent to the injustices of the status quo. May it be a journey to radical discipleship for those ready to take on the invitation and challenge offered by Jesus.

And, in the end, may you, too, give others hope.

Bishop Karen P. Oliveto
Denver, Colorado
September 26, 2019

INTRODUCTION

This book is for the queer kids. It's for people who wrestle with whether or not they can stay in the churches that raised them. It's for those who mourn the Church's failure to engage with social justice, and who have been told by a church that their identity is wrong or "incompatible with Christian teaching."[1] It's also for those leaders who have worked for decades to make their churches safe spaces for the LGBTQ+ community. This book is for all of us who hear the word *church* and instantly think of debate, exclusion, injustice, and fear.

Maybe you've written off church completely, but you know deep within your bones that *these injustices cannot be what God intended the church to be.* If that uncomfortable gnawing on your spirit has brought you here—if that voice in your head keeps saying, "Something's got to change"— then maybe you have an inner conviction to see the Church become more than it is. Maybe, just maybe, we've been called to reclaim the very idea of what church is and who is allowed in—together.

Even though many of us queer kids have called churches

our homes, some denominations don't allow us to be who we are, to be ordained as pastors or our marriages to be celebrated in church buildings simply because of whom we love or how we identify. Some people in my church claim to welcome me, but will not recognize the deep commitment and love I have for my partner, and the love I have for God. Some people will welcome me into their pews but not behind their pulpits—this is not a welcome, but rather an invitation to second-class citizenship. Some say they love us because they "love the sinner, hate the sin." For us queer kids, that's impossible because what they believe is our "sin" is inseparable from who we are. We are who God has created us to be—beautifully queer children—and there's no sin in that.

The institutional Church (that's the capital C) has used God's name to exclude groups of people throughout history and has instigated the deaths and suicides of so many. And so, you might ask me why I persist. Why do I stay in an institution that continually harms me and many other groups of people—especially queer people, people of color, and women in ministry? Maybe you feel this same tension and you're ready to leave.

For me, it all started at a microphone with a three-minute speech at a global gathering of The United Methodist Church. Since I'm not at a microphone or under a timer anymore, this book is my response. These words are my vision and hope for the future, an invitation to action for each of us. We can join together and begin reclaiming what church is from the harmful hands of fundamentalism. We—the religious rejects—can be the church, and we have the opportunity to reclaim what it means to be a Christian today. Together, we can reclaim church as a place of justice-seeking, loving, and passionate people who are actively creating heaven on Earth for all.

THE SPEECH

I walked to the microphone, and I could feel my body shivering with nerves. My chest was tight, and it was getting hard to breathe. Thousands of eyes suddenly looked at me, and I wasn't sure what to say. I wish I could have shared my story—my journey as a gay Christian who feels called to ministry—in a more private setting, but I didn't get that chance. For some reason, *that* was the moment, and my life has been forever changed because of it.

It was February 25, 2019, and voting delegates from United Methodist churches around the world had gathered in St. Louis. We sat in a football stadium, and despite the tables and chairs, the mood in the arena still felt like a competition. Tables and chairs had been added to the field so that it would feel less like a brutal competition. It didn't. Our task was to decide whether or not our Church around the world would allow queer people to be ordained as pastors and married in our churches. This was a Special Conference. Usually we meet every four years and discuss topics like education or our efforts in combating malaria, but this time we met for the sole purpose of deciding whether or not our Church would include people like me. It's a painful thing to have people around the world discuss whether or not you should exist, or at least whether or not you can serve God, but that was the purpose there.

I was still a senior in college, and I was a reserve delegate from the Upper New York area (that's an area of about eight hundred churches in upstate New York—all of New York excluding New York City). Being a reserve delegate meant that I didn't go on the floor of the conference (where the voting members sat) unless another delegate from my conference needed a break. "Put me in, coach," is what I wanted to say as I sat in the stadium seating high up above. As more than eight hundred people from all parts of the world decided my fate, I had to sit and watch from the balcony. Maybe you did watch the conference, or you've experienced moments like this where the people around you talk about part of who you are without ever talking about you as a human being, or with you as an equal. It's tough, but it's helpful to know that we're not alone in this feeling.

It was the evening of the twenty-fifth, the second-to-last day of the conference, and it wasn't going well. Those who wanted to keep us queer people out of the pulpits and wedding chapels were getting their way. People were saying horrible things about "homosexuals" and aggressively arguing with one another in an international spotlight. The Bible was being used to justify the exclusion of LGBTQ+ folks, and Christians weren't acting very Christlike. It was ugly and heavy, and it was the top law-making body of my Church.

It was on this evening, as it seemed like our Church was ending and only a couple of queer people got a chance to talk, that one of the delegates from my area sent me a text. "If the plans about LGBTQ+ inclusion come up again, you can take my seat." He continued, "Our church is falling apart anyways, so it won't make a difference whether you're up there or down here." It didn't sound very hopeful, and it seemed too late for the plans to come up again anyway. But I sent back, "OK, thanks."

The plans about inclusion did come up, just as the day was ending—and I got the text: "Hurry. Come take my seat." My heart started to thump in my throat, and I quickly looked around. I was sitting next to a sweet older woman from my area who had been cracking jokes all weekend to keep my spirits up. "Shirley, will you watch my bags? I'm going on the floor!" She smiled with her big grandmother smile and said, "Sure, honey! Get down there."

I sprinted down two escalators, checked in at two security checkpoints, and ran to the table where they gave me a voting device. I was out of breath and frantically checking my phone to see where the other guy was. "I'm here. Where are you?" I texted and impatiently peeked through the doorway into the conference. Just then, he walked in and the folks at the table deactivated his card and activated mine.

I tried to play it cool as I emerged from the doorway

and onto the vast arena floor. The lights were bright, and it felt like everyone was looking at me (even though they weren't). I quickly walked to the table where delegates from my area were sitting. "Hey, we're glad you're here," one of them whispered. I sat down, took a breath, and pushed the little gray button on my voting device to speak.

I had no idea at all what I would say, but I knew I had to say something. There were people who had their "speak" button pressed for days but were never called on, so my hopes still weren't high. And yet somehow, for some reason, within five minutes of getting that text, running down, scanning in, sitting down, and pressing my button, I heard the moderator say, "J. J. Warren. Speech for the motion. Microphone 1."

I felt paralyzed. I didn't expect to be called on, and now I was asked to go to a microphone in front of bishops and older church leaders, people from around the world, and say something that made sense. I was supposed to say something to help them see us as humans, as God's beautifully created children. If I could have disappeared, I would have. In that moment and in front of thousands of people, I stood to speak without having a single word prepared beforehand. I first had to state the reason for my speech, which was to refer one of the plans about inclusion to Judicial Council (our version of the Supreme Court) to ensure that it could be passed without being deemed "unconstitutional." I had three minutes to say why this mattered, but I didn't have thirty seconds' worth of anything to say.

Then, all of a sudden, I began to share my story.

Only now, after watching the video each time I visit a church, could I repeat what I said. I watch and I don't recognize myself; I'm not usually someone who raises my voice, or cries in public. I don't usually stand unprepared before thousands of people. And yet, in that moment, that's exactly what God called me to do: pour forth my soul; lay open my heart, passion, and pain before these people; and cry for mercy before the Church.

"And as someone who has grown up in our Church, and as someone who is gay, and goes to the least-religious college in the US—my evangelism has grown." I felt overwhelmed with emotion as I thought of the people on my campus who were told by their churches that they had to change who they were or leave. As I thought about this, I started to shout,

> They didn't know God could love them *because their churches said God didn't*! . . . And so, if we can be a church that brings Jesus to people who are told they can't be loved, that's what I want our church to be, and that's the Methodist Church that I love and that I want to be a pastor in one day. . . . We are the church together! This is the body of Christ! We are God's children! Let us be the church together!

I felt completely bare, like every bit of life I had in me was released into that moment. The people in the stands and the delegates on the floor erupted into shouts and cheers, and even our bishops stood in support as the conference crumbled into emotional chaos. It was the most vulnerable I've ever felt, but the messages I received in the weeks and months after have made it all worthwhile. Mothers of queer children have written to say they're sorry for treating their children poorly, and that they'll try to rebuild relationships with them. Queer kids have said they gained the confidence to come out to their churches and families. Even older LGBTQ+ folks have said that they finally felt like they had a voice in the Church. One unplanned speech by a college kid from a small town in rural upstate New York was able to create space for queer religious folks.

But I know that one speech doesn't turn the tide of religious culture, and that one person isn't a movement. The truth is, the only reason I was able to be there is because people have been working for decades to reclaim the whole idea of church—to make it a place where queer people and people of color and immigrants and the differently abled can find refuge and a home. The struggle for inclusion has been a long one, and it still has far to go—but we're each making a difference. Each of us has the opportunity to find joy in our God-given identities and claim the sacred space of church as our place of worship too. For generations, folks have put their lives on the line for us, facing religious persecution for whom they've been created to love or for the gender they identify with. It's our turn, the young religious rejects of every color and country whom churches continue to condemn, to rise up and continue the journey toward the promised land of inclusion for all.

PLANNING THE REVOLUTION

To start reclaiming anything, we have to explore what it was meant to be and when or how it was hijacked from its original meaning. We have to go back to the beginning. In the first chapter, I'll explore the question, *Who is God?* This is no small question, and I don't claim authority to give *the* answer. What I hope to offer is a beginning, a starting point for each of us to question once again who we have experienced God to be, and the role of the Bible in creating different images of God. Many of us have grown up with images, almost like cold marble statues, of who God is, and these statues cause us pain. My hope is that you'll gain the confidence to chisel away at the harmful statues of God and learn some basic choreography to start your dance with the Divine. Asking *who is God* should be an exciting and personal journey, and my hope is that we can each dance in safety, knowing that our partner doesn't actually plan for us to "burn in hell" for being who we are.

The next step in the great religious revolution is reclaiming Scripture, aka "the Bible." If we think of the Church as a house, we can't just go in swinging and knock down every wall. The Bible is like the support beams of a house, so we're going to take apart the surface-level "Bible says" statements that have been plastered over the beams and used against us queer Christians, and we're going to search for the truth that lies beneath. It's not so easy to say "The Bible tells me so" when we're dealing with a collection of books that has been edited, translated, and compiled over thousands of years. In chapter 2, we'll take a closer look at the "clobber" passages, the ones that are used against queer Christians, and we'll carefully take them apart. My goal is not to tear apart the Bible or get rid of it—just the opposite. Once we see past the harmful things that other people have told us it says, we can discover for ourselves a deeper understanding of Scripture, one that has brought me closer to God.

The process of reclaiming Church, like reclaiming an identity like gay or queer, is a personal one. We each go through it at our own pace and in our own ways—but we don't have to go through it alone. In chapter 3, "Born This Way," I'll share some of my coming-out story and what it was like for me to reclaim my God-given identity. Before I came out, I often felt like I was wearing a costume that someone else constructed. I was trying my best to hide my sexuality and be the person everyone thought I should be. In that chapter, we'll take a look at these costumes, and my hope is that you'll gain the confidence to tear through yours—if not in front of everyone, then maybe in front of the mirror. You are loved just as you are, and you're born this way for a reason. Let's figure out that reason, and use our queerness as a gift to the world and to the Church.

Finally, after searching the depths of God's identity, dismantling the harmful uses of Scripture, and coming to embrace our true selves, it's time for us to boldly say, "*We are the Church!*" My hope is that this book will be your tool kit, that you'll be able to reclaim your own identity as well as that of the church. In this final chapter, we'll get down to business about what it means to be church, what church meant to the ancients, and what it can be for us today. It's your turn to take action and enact what we've studied together. As religious rejects around the globe, my hope is that we are inspired to reclaim church together. We can bring a queer revival and revolution of the Church; we can warm hearts, open minds, and embrace folks as they are. We truly are the Church, and it's time we take the baton from previous generations and run together toward the promised land of inclusion for all. Welcome to the revolution.

Note

1. ¶ 304.3 from *The Book of Discipline of The United Methodist Church, 2016*. Copyright © 2016 by The United Methodist Publishing House. Used by permission.

Chapter 1

WHO IS GOD?

It's time to dance. When we think about God, it should be an experience—an intimate tango with our soulmate or a mosh pit of joy with our friends. We can try to learn some choreography from the Bible, but this dance is active and ongoing, and it's unique for each of us. My awkward and clumsy dance with God will look different from yours, and that's fine. So, whatever you were told about God before, let it go. Release the tension in your fists as you read this and feel the chains around you fall. You have every right to experience God in your own way. Take everything you were ever told or just took for granted, and say, "Goodbye," because right now we're starting fresh. It's day one for all of us.

For a long time, my idea of God was based on what I heard other people say. I had this whole "macho masculine" image in my mind, the God who sent plagues and turned people to salt. I heard people talk about "Him" and "His judgment" or "His power." Don't get me wrong, my home church was full of kind-hearted older ladies who acted as everyone's mothers. I was lucky. Even in this church, though, that idea of a masculine God hid under the surface of every conversation; we just assumed that's who God was. The problem with repeating what our parents' generation has told us is that they're just repeating what they heard from their parents, and those people repeated the ones before them, and so on. It's time we end the cycle. No more repetition just because that's the way it's always been. It's time to start making some decisions for ourselves. Sometimes my image of God seems like a rigid marble statue whose cold eyes look at me with judgment. It's time to take that dusty statue of God and smash it.

That might be a little dramatic, but you get the point, right? Starting now, we have to find out for ourselves who God *really* is—and who God isn't. Chances are, if you're reading this book then at some point you've been told that God can't love you the way you are—that something about you needs to change. Maybe being rejected by Christians changed the way you think about God. Lord knows even now, after being out of the closet since my first year of college, I still hear those voices: "Your love is a sin," "It's a choice," and "Repent, you sodomite." This last delightful comment was whispered into my ear by an older woman after I preached in Upstate New York. This is why we have to start from the beginning—to reclaim God before we reclaim church. We have to deconstruct what everyone else has forced upon us and rediscover who God is for ourselves—and for others who aren't quite there yet. It's time to start discovering our own dance with God.

Somehow, I've always believed that there is a God and that this God loves me no matter what, but I know that not everyone feels that way. Not everyone entered high school and got a hippie pastor like mine, someone who made our church come out of the closet. Not everyone experienced the parts of Christianity that have filled me with joy, like summer camp and youth group. For some people, even the words *Christian*, *church*, and *God* are triggers. These words can remind us of dark places—of sitting alone in our rooms feeling unlovable. I was privileged by the church I grew up in, and even though I didn't feel comfortable enough to come out in my hometown, my church was not a place that preached exclusion. But I didn't just get lucky; people around me spoke up. Now it's our turn.

FINDING THE RHYTHM, NOT THE STATUE

I'm about to sound like a proper southern lady, but I love my Bible. It's very special to me and I read it often. Here's the thing I don't think many Christians are comfortable saying, though: *you're allowed to love the Bible and be critical of it.* It's like playfully teasing a member of your family; it's OK if you do it, but it gets under your skin if someone else does. I believe that the biblical writers were inspired by God. I know, however, that the books that make up the Protestant Bible (that's the one most people read who aren't Catholic) were written at specific times with specific people in mind. Don't get me wrong, there are universal themes that can guide people of all generations, like the "golden rule" (Matthew 7:12) or "love your neighbor" (Mark 12:31; Leviticus 19:18).

A majority of the Bible, however, requires an understanding of the historical context in order for the laws, family systems, and assumptions about God to make sense—like not wearing clothing of mixed fabrics (Leviticus 19:19). All of these books were edited by many different editors over centuries. I have a great editor who asks questions when I'm not clear. Sometimes, she crosses out entire paragraphs or suggests that I move chapter 2 to chapter 4. Sure, she's usually right, but if the biblical editors were anything like her, imagine how much has changed. Can we really claim to know exactly who God is if we rely solely on a collection of books that have been edited countless times?

The ancient Hebrew people believed that God caused the big flood that washed away most of their land. To them, God must have destroyed the entire earth, but why? The fact is, the flood didn't destroy the entire earth, and we have evidence to prove it. This doesn't mean the Bible is a lie; *it means we're reading it the wrong way*. If we read the Bible as a history book filled with facts, we're going to have a rough time trying to make sense of it. But, if we read it with the understanding that it's a collection of stories that are trying to reveal a deeper truth, then we begin to experience the dance rather than viewing an ancient, unchanging statue. We have to wonder what all of the books were trying to get at. What's the underlying message? If the ancient people thought the flood was from God as a punishment—what for? Maybe they said to each other, "Hey, something's not right here. People are killing each other and that can't be the way God intended for us to live." So, when a flood came around the same time that they were questioning their actions, they thought it was from God.

Were they wrong? I don't know, but I don't think that's the point. When I read the Bible, I look at each book with this question in mind: *What does it tell me about the people's understanding of who God is?* The people who wrote about the flood thought that whatever they were doing was against God's will, which means it was contrary to who they believed God to be. A good God wouldn't will something evil, right? Just before the flood, Genesis 6:11 says, "Now the earth was corrupt in God's sight, and the earth was filled with violence." It seems like the early people thought violence and corruption were things that were contrary to God's will, and if God doesn't will us to be violent, why would God be violent? If the people thought that violence was contrary to who God was, then why did they assume that God would use more violence to end their violence? This just doesn't add up. It's the sort of question I'd hate to get from a Sunday school kid because there's no easy answer.

Maybe the people had a good idea of God's values, but they were less clear about how far God would go to enforce them. This is just a theory, but it doesn't seem too far off—especially in the stories of Abraham, Lot, and Gomorrah. In Genesis 18:22-33, God and Abraham had an intense debate. We'll talk more about Sodom and Gomorrah in the next chapter, but for now, it's important to know that the Bible says nothing about Sodom and Gomorrah being destroyed because the people were gay. It *does* say that the people were arrogant, greedy, and apathetic (Ezekiel 16:48-49). Because of their lack of care for the needy, God said, "Let me go down there and teach these people a lesson" (that is, rain down fire and destroy them all). Abraham, however, thought mass murder couldn't be right. What if there were good people down there? So, he approached God and said, "Whoa, whoa, whoa, wait a minute, God. What if there are fifty righteous people in the city? Will you destroy them too?" (I'm paraphrasing a little.) And God said, "Dang, good point. If there are fifty righteous people, then I guess I'll save everybody" (Genesis 18:26, paraphrased). Abraham kept going and pushing this logic to the extremes. "Well, what if there are forty-five . . . or forty . . . or thirty . . . or twenty . . . or ten righteous people?!" And God said, "Fine, if there are ten righteous people, I'll save them all" (Genesis 18:32, paraphrased). Debate settled.

Or was it? I don't think we can take this story literally, and it probably tells us more about the authors' internal struggle with morality than it tells us about God. I mean, how did Abraham approach God in the first place? This is a perfect example of why we have to dance and feel the rhythm, the underlying truth, rather than keep staring at that marble statue of literalism. The authors knew that disregarding the poor, apathy, and violence were contrary to who God was, but they still weren't sure how far God would go to make sure God's will was enforced. Would God wipe out an entire city—even if some of them were "righteous"? The writers were on a search to figure out who God was, and in the meantime, they debated whether God would burn an entire city even of good folks who acted well but lived among those who didn't. Was this actually a conversation that occurred between God and Abraham? Maybe, but maybe not. Instead of debating whether this happened or not, we can look behind the scenes and see that even the biblical writers were unsure about who God is and how God carries out justice. They were engaged in the dance, and passages like this one invite us to step in as well. What do you think God would do?

Now that was a lot of assumption-smashing material crammed into a few pages. Maybe you feel like everything you've ever believed has been called into question and you want to throw this book down and get some fresh air—that's OK. This awkward and uncomfortable space is exactly where we need to be if we're going to truly set aside everything we've heard before and start fresh. What I hope you got out of this is that the statue of God that we each hold in our mind has been carved and created by the way other people have interpreted these ancient stories for us. The stories aren't wrong, but they're also not complete. I don't believe that God suddenly stopped inspiring people or that God vanished out of the blue.

The books of the Bible provide insights into how the ancient God-followers experienced God, and they leave space for us to continue to experience God today. These stories are a good place to start, and they guide us through the beginning steps, but the dance is only just beginning. This can feel overwhelming, but no one said that rethinking thousands of years of history and interpretation would be easy. And besides, we're in this together. Now, let's dance.

GOD'S NOT A MACHO MAN

First of all, let's say who God isn't. Maybe God isn't someone you want to deal with. Maybe God has been made out to be some vengeful tyrant who was obviously a white guy with a nice beard. But maybe, deep in the depths of who you are, some part of you knew this couldn't be true. Even if we think something must be wrong—especially something as enormous as the identity of God—hearing it over and over again makes an impression on us. It's hard work to deconstruct an idea of Her, especially one we've heard for years. This why people have gotten away with doing horrible things in God's name. They've been able to use this false statue of God, which has been passed down from one generation to the next, to justify their cruelty as "the will of God." Depending on what image of God someone has in their head, he or she can justify all sorts of harm. This is why we have to smash the statue.

Let's be clear: God's not a scary macho man in the sky. God's not even a person. Maybe you thought it was weird earlier when I used *Her* as God's pronoun. I thought it was weird when I first heard it. I'm not saying God's a woman, and I'm not saying God's a man either. The truth is, we're not really sure what God is other than, well, God. In Hebrew, every word—even *house* or *table*—is either masculine or feminine; there's no neutral gender. So, it's true, most references to God are masculine, but that's because it was the default (and I totally agree that this is problematic and patriarchal).

Many Hebrew verbs are masculine and then a feminine ending is added to them. Even though the masculine was the "go-to" gender, there were plenty of references to God as feminine. In Deuteronomy 32:18, for example, God is described as "the God who gave you birth." In Isaiah 66:13, God says, through the prophet, "As a mother comforts her child, / so I will comfort you." In Matthew 23:37, Jesus says, "I desired to gather your children together as a hen gathers her brood under her wings." So, is God a woman? No. Is God a man? No (unless we're talking about Jesus). What we can say is that God is not confined to a gender.

Have you ever seen Michelangelo's painting "The Creation of Adam"? It's exactly what I'm talking about: God is a big white guy with a majestic beard and a flowing robe. Clearly this image tells us more about the people who have been making decisions for the Church than it does about God. Do you think a queer black woman created that image? No. So, our idea of who God is has been sculpted by the people who have held power in the Church and in society, and then "gifted" it down to us. It's not just sloppy theology, it's racist, sexist, homophobic, ableist—and it can't be who God is.

So, now that we've taken the first whack with our hammer to the rigidly defined muscular white guy statue of God, the image in your mind might have changed. Mine did. Engraved in that old statue of God was the exclusion of queer kids like us, and the "evidence" that God obviously wasn't black. That statue is of a God who would rain fire and cause a flood, who only let men lead. But that's not the God I've experienced—or even the God I find in the space between the written verses.

GOD'S NOT ANGRY

One of the churches I visited last summer was deep in the city of Rochester, and it looked pretty rough around the edges. The cement ramp that led to the main door was cracked all over, and the paint was peeling on every side. Inside, the sanctuary was dark. Chairs were lined up against the walls, and the altar area was filled with furniture they no longer used. Honestly, it looked abandoned—but that's sort of what they were going for. I had never seen a church like this, and I wasn't sure how I felt about it. It was dirty and hot, but it had that deep spiritual feeling—the kind you get when you stand on a mountain and watch the sunset or see the ocean for the first time.

The pastor came around the corner, and if I've ever felt out of place, it was then. He was one of those cool pastors who didn't have to try. He wasn't "cool" as in someone who wears skinny jeans to try to look younger or say things like, "I'm down with that." He wore a dirty flannel, a gray beanie, and sandals. Meanwhile, I stood there in my pink sport coat and white-washed skinny jeans. I thought to myself, "Dang, I bet Jesus would look more like this guy." This wasn't the church or the pastor I was used to, but it definitely was a church and he was the pastor.

We sat in his office, which doubled as the nursery, and started talking about the needs we saw in the progressive Christian community. At some point, God's jealousy came up. He leaned back in an old green chair and said, "I know some foster kids who have never felt like they mattered to anybody. So, when they hear that God is jealous for them, it means for once in their lives they matter to someone." He paused and looked out of the window as if something in the overgrown weeds outside held the answers. "The Ivy League kids get all nervous when we talk about God's wrath or jealousy," he said, his eyes shifting back to me, "but it matters."

I have to admit, I was a little thrown off. Wrath and jealousy have always been a conservative thing in my mind—it was how *they* said God acted toward people like us. But maybe this non-ironic hipster pastor had a point; maybe God's jealousy and wrath do matter. For now, I'll say that God is not one-dimensional. If God acts wrathful or jealous, it doesn't mean that God *is* wrathful or jealous. I can get angry and yell at a microphone, but it doesn't mean I'm an angry person. I'm usually the opposite. I like to help people resolve conflicts and keep peace. No one is defined by an emotion—especially God.

But like I said before, the stories about God's wrath (like Abraham's great debate with God) tell us more about the authors' attempts to dance with God than they do about how God might actually act. If God's not a human, then God probably knows everything that will happen in the universe. She has *foreknowledge*. But I don't believe that God is a puppet master who pulls strings or chose Trump as president. In my dance, God knows what steps I'll take, but She doesn't make me take them. It doesn't make complete sense, and we could go on and on, but these are things that we each have to dance with. We each have to find our own way of exploring who God is and how God acts. I don't believe any one person has all the answers.

The point is that I don't believe God is angry or jealous—it's just too human. Humanizing God, or *anthropomorphizing* Her, is helpful because we're able to relate better. If we can picture God crying with us, it feels like we can understand each other. But this has its limitations, and one of those is that if we see God as human, we start to believe it as well—and we begin to limit who God is. God becomes someone who is easily understood and who clearly hates gays, is white, and thinks women should sit quietly. Hopefully you've seen that this isn't true; it's what the cisgender (that means people who identify with the gender they were born with) straight white men who ran the Church told us God is. Besides, if God knows everything that will happen, why would She get angry when it happens? God is greater than anger or jealousy, but these emotions can help us to relate to God and try to understand Her will.

GOD'S WILL

If we go back to these stories and try to understand *what* the authors thought would make God angry, it helps us to understand their perception of God's will. In the story of Abraham and Sodom and Gomorrah, pride, violence, apathy, and excess were contrary to the will of God. To the authors, these things made God angry. Because they could say, "See, God is angered by these injustices," they were able to influence the community in an effort to change their ways. What better way to stop people from reckless behaviors than saying that God would rain fire down and destroy them all? They used the will of God to influence others, but this isn't always a bad thing.

Today, we can do the same thing—but without giving God human emotions. We could say that the exploitative nature of US capitalism is contrary to God's will. We can call other Christians to action by saying, "If we want to follow God, we can't be complacent in this system that targets minority groups through excessive pharmaceutical pricing." In this case, we've used the will of God to motivate others in creating a more equitable world. Our understanding of God's will informs our understanding of who God is. If exploitation is against, and apathy toward those in poverty is contrary to, the will of God, then that means our God must be a lover of the "lowly" and a great equalizer. Our interpretation of God's will profoundly impacts our understanding of God's character.

We can apply the meaning of ancient biblical stories to our situations today without continuing the myth of God the angry macho man. We can reclaim God and these stories by separating the character of God from the actions the authors describe. The injustices committed by the people in Genesis 18 motivated God to act because they were contrary to Her will. But God's actions depict a God whose character is angry, indecisive, and vengeful. We can believe that the injustices committed were against God's will without believing that the way God acted is fact. We have to engage in the dance for ourselves.

I believe that violence is contrary to who God is, so it doesn't make sense in my dance for God to suddenly get violent in an effort to end violence. If God is good, and God's will is good, God could not achieve creating a good world through evil means. God wouldn't use violence to end violence. We each have to keep dancing and question how God would respond—but that's a whole other book. For now, I hope you feel empowered to use these ancient stories in your dance. Try out the old steps to some new music. Pretty soon, our dancing will attract others, and they'll want to dance with us as well.

GOD IS LOVE

God is love, and those who abide in love abide in God, and God abides in them.

1 John 4:16

It might be cheesy, but one of my favorite verses from the Bible is 1 John 4:16. It sounds like something sappy I'd read in a Hallmark card, but it's actually in the Bible. The thing is, it's not just cute, it's powerful. It offers us a new way to read the Bible and a new soundtrack to dance to. Not only that, it changes who our dance partner is and how They interact with us (here I'm using "They" as a non-gendered pronoun for God). When I read, "God is love," I don't assume that that's it. Well, God is love and that's sweet—right? No. This verse offers us something much more open and creative than just a simple answer; it leaves us room to dance.

Think back to God and Abraham's battle of wits in Genesis 18. We have a city full of people who are neglecting the poor, not offering hospitality to travelers from foreign lands, living lavishly, and full of big egos. Then, we have authors who want us to know that these things are contrary to God's will. Now, put on your love lens. This love lens is like our Sherlock Holmes magnifying glass that lets us see things we never noticed.

You should see a city where people at the bottom are being exploited by people at the top. If God is love, are they living in the presence of God? No. Are they obeying God's will? No. Their dance is like a line dance, but one in which only a certain type of people is allowed to join in. So, the God of love intervenes. Even though the authors might have gotten it wrong—even though they wrote about fire raining down—at the very heart of it all, they were attempting to describe a God who deeply cares for humanity and all of creation. They were trying to reconcile and dance with a God who opposes injustice—but they didn't know how She would deal with it. Deep down they knew God loved them, but they didn't know how God showed Her love. They got Her will right, but they damaged Her character.

Maybe the God you grew up with is not a God who acts out of love, and maybe that makes believing in this God hard to accept. Like me, maybe you're wondering where this lovey-dovey God was while the people at your church or school called you a fag and used the Bible against you. I told my Twitter followers about the harmful statue of the God I knew, and I invited them to share theirs too. One man replied that the statue he grew up with was, "*The one that said that I must not love him enough because I haven't changed.*" Another woman responded, "*I literally thought of God as Hitler in the sky. . . . No grace. I had no future because the world was ending and none of my hopes, dreams, or aspirations mattered.*" A fellow queer friend of mine responded, "*It's difficult for me to separate an entire*

decade of people telling me that I'm not worthy of God."
This is the God that many of us have been threatened with.
This doesn't sound like the God of 1 John.

It's not easy to face our triggers, so I'm glad you've
stuck around this long. The truth is, this lovey-dovey
God isn't the one many churches preach. So, if you feel
like you're meeting Her for the first time, that's probably
because you are. It's a difficult task for us religious rejects:
to not only face the One who was used to damn us but also
to find love and compassion in this same being under the
same name. When the people who have excluded us say
that God is love, it dismisses the pain they've caused us
using God's own name. But when we say that God is love,
it's a call to action.

GOD'S AN ACTIVIST

If anything, God's a tree-hugging feminist who marches
at Pride and sings "Kumbaya" around a campfire with
gluten-free marshmallows. God's saving the elephants in
Kenya or chained to a bulldozer at the edge of a forest in
South America. God's standing outside the White House
with a sign that says "No More Drone Strikes" while
wearing a pink hat from the Women's March. God has
always been on the side of the oppressed—liberating slaves
from Egypt or reaching out to touch the "unclean." God's
always been an activist, instigating social, political, and
religious change—and God still is. This is what love looks
like; this is what love does.

The question facing Christians today shouldn't be whether or not God is on the side of migrants; it should be, "Why aren't we already on their side?" In Genesis 11, the people of the earth had come together and begun to focus their energies on building a tower—one that would reach the heavens. We could talk more about towers being inherently hierarchical, but for right now, the point is that God scattered the people. The people were living in one place and speaking one language, and yet God made them migrants and altered their one language into many. To be a migrant and to speak a different language, if we believe this story, is a direct result of God's actions.

In the next chapter, Genesis 12, God calls Abraham to a different life—a life that would be difficult but would mean that his children would be the ones God cared for. Abraham would become the founder of faith, the father of all, but before all of this happened, God called Abraham to be a migrant: "Go from your country and your kindred and your father's house to the land that I will show you" (Genesis 12:1). How can we sit by as countries like ours oppress the very people God used to do great things? The entire book of Exodus—and the rest of the Torah (that's the first five books of the Bible)—details the travels and trials of the Hebrew people as they migrated out of Egypt's oppression in search of better treatment. Migration is part of our story.

The Bible doesn't just support migrants, it looks out for the disabled and residents from other countries. In the book of Leviticus, the people are instructed not to "revile the deaf or put a stumbling block before the blind" (Leviticus 19:14). It tells them, "When an alien resides with you in your land, you shall not oppress the alien. . . . You shall love the alien as yourself" (Leviticus 19:33-34). God is—and always has been—the God of the alien, the differently-abled, and the oppressed. Somehow, that old statue of God as the angry guy who looks suspiciously similar to the powerful people got pretty popular. It's tempting to just walk away from the corruption, misuse, and misinterpretation—to admit that church is a lost cause. Sometimes, it feels like it'd be easier to just walk away from God and church altogether. But I know that the marble statue isn't an accurate representation of who God is. We've spent a lot of time hammering away at it and learning to dance around the pieces, but I don't just want to play defense or smash everyone's old statues. I want to dance, and I want all of us to dance together in our own ways as one big celebration—as the true Church.

LOVE CASTS OUT FEAR

A lot of people say that hate is the opposite of love, but my gray-bearded Bible professor at Sarah Lawrence said otherwise. One night, as most of us were staring with glassy eyes, he asked, "In the story of Genesis, when is it that the people separate themselves from God?" He paused and looked around the table, making eye contact with each of us before saying, "It's when they felt fear and, subsequently, shame."

After Eve and Adam ate from the "tree of the knowledge of good and evil," God decided to stop by and take a stroll through the garden (Genesis 2:9; 3:8). "But the LORD God called to the man, and said to him, 'Where are you?' He [the man] said, 'I heard the sound of you in the garden, and I was afraid, because I was naked; and I hid myself' " (Genesis 3:9-10). God knew the people were naked the whole time, but God didn't care. When the people saw themselves for the first time, they felt shame and this shame caused them to be terrified of what God might do, so they tried to hide from God. When they looked at each other, when they truly saw what they were, they were horrified that God couldn't love them—but God knew the whole time.

Fear keeps us from loving God, and it keeps us from loving ourselves. If God is love, it means that those churches and "religious" people who make us feel ashamed for being ourselves are not sharing God. Yup, I said it. If their teachings don't help us to love ourselves, love others, love the world around us, and love God back, then their teachings aren't about God. They might be staring at that statue, but they're not dancing with the true God. As the Psalm reads:

> I praise you, for I am fearfully and wonderfully made.
>
> Wonderful are your works;
> that I know very well.
>
> My frame was not hidden from you,
> when I was being made in secret,

intricately woven in the depths of the earth.
Your eyes beheld my unformed substance.

Psalm 139:14-16

We are wonderfully made. We are brushstrokes in God's universal masterpiece, and we are very good. God knew us before we had bodies—and God knew we were good. Hear that. Take it in. *You are good.* God loves you because that's who God is and it's who you are. We have been created out of love, everything about us—yes, even our queerness—and God loves us for it. Though the Church may have filled us with shame, though we may have written off God out of fear, we are loved and nothing will ever change that. Our dance partner is patiently waiting, and we can take Their hand whenever we're ready. There's no need to fear God or our true selves any longer because God's love for us casts out even this fear. It's time to let God in and love ourselves in the process.

LOVE IS ACTIVE

Next, we have to love others. I don't mean the surface-level, "Hello, how are you?" Jean Valjean sang it best in *Les Misérables*, "To love another person is to see the face of God." We can't just be nice; we have to see God in everyone. If we looked at everyone we passed on the sidewalk or on the train and saw God in them—if we recognized their inherent goodness as well as our own—we'd be living in a very different world. It'd be a world where people like us don't have to read books like this because no one would be told they don't belong. It would be a world where suicides ceased, and children were set free from slavery—where we didn't judge folks by the color of their skin or by their gender expression. To say that God is love means to radically change the way our families, our neighbors, and the Church act and interact. It means a rediscovery of what it means to be Christian—a deconstruction of the angry white dude and a reclaiming of the God who is first and foremost love itself.

There is a God, and They love you because that's just who They are. So, take your time. If a sledgehammer isn't your thing, it's OK to slowly chisel away at who you were told God is. It's a process. And when you're ready, God's there to take your hand and celebrate in the dance with you.

Chapter 2

THE BIBLE TELLS ME WHAT?

When I was five years old, my family moved from Ft. Lauderdale, Florida, to a small town in Upstate New York. It was a big adjustment—especially in the winter. Our first winter there, we had the heat set to 80 degrees (that was before we realized how much heating costs). Before we moved in, though, the house was a real piece of work. On top of that, since I'm one of seven kids, a lot of work had to be done to fit us all wherever we moved. When we first looked at the house, I remember seeing a dead bird in the kitchen, an old stepladder leading nowhere, and a huge wall that divided the room in half. The kitchen was tiny and so was the dining room because of that wall. So, my family decided that it had to come down.

I was little and the thought of tearing down a wall sounded pretty cool. I thought they'd let all seven of us go at it with hammers. I thought wrong. Apparently, you can't just start whacking through a wall without doing some homework first. There are pipes and wires and beams that you're not supposed to mess with—especially as a five-year-old. We never got to do any of the hammering, but I watched the construction folks a few times. I noticed that even though they were taking the wall down, they were careful to leave the things that were necessary—like the support beams. First, they had to understand the old wall, then they could take apart the pieces that were in the way.

There are things about the Church that remind me of that wall. Sometimes there are things in the Church that get in the way of relationships and create barriers. Maybe you want to take a sledgehammer to the whole idea of church—there are times when I wish I could. But there are some elements that are necessary to keep, things about the church that I think are important to hold on to as we redesign the blueprints to make more space. Scripture (aka "the Bible") is one of those things. Scripture is like the support beams that hold everything up. Rather than whack right through them and move on, let's carefully deconstruct the verses that "exclusive Christians" use to build their walls and keep us LGBTQ+ folks from participating in churches.

Taking apart these verses doesn't mean that the entire Bible is a lie, or that it's no good to us at all. In fact, it's the opposite. We're taking off all of the garbage that people have plastered over the beams of Scripture—all the decades of mistranslations and misuses—and we're tossing it out to show the truth underneath. This is an extraordinary task, and it'll take a lot of us—all over the world—to do this. What we're doing is not only taking apart harmful uses of Scripture but also building up a Church from what we find underneath—a Church where everyone belongs and dances together. I believe that we religious rejects can build this Church together, and we'll all have a place in it.

THE LETTER

Back in high school, I was deep in the closet. Being gay was like seeing Bigfoot: it was just a myth. There was one gay kid who moved to town, but most people stayed away from him. In middle school, I thought I liked girls, but by high school I knew I didn't—I just didn't know why. I tried to have girlfriends like everybody else, but I never wanted to kiss them—so that didn't work. There weren't any gay couples in town or role models to look up to. If two women kissed on an episode of "Grey's Anatomy" while my family was watching, my parents made us cover our eyes. Back then, I thought being gay wasn't normal, and it definitely wasn't something I could be. At the same time, deep within me I knew I was different. I thought it was a temptation, a defect, or that I was straying from the way things should be. I must have been a bad seed. In my mind, no one was "gay," they were just choosing the wrong thing. It was around this time that a new pastor came to our church.

In my senior year of high school, the new pastor began to preach about LGBTQ+ inclusion for the first time. That didn't go over well in my small town. People got angry, and some left the church altogether. When the pastor wore a rainbow-colored stole, even my dad wanted to leave.

There was this one person, though, who was so upset that he or she decided to respond in classic church fashion: to write a letter and post it where everyone could see. The church bulletin board was that place. The board was one of those wall-sized corkboards that had hundreds of thumb tacks and looked like it had been around since the 1970s. One thing you should know about older church people: the bulletin board is essentially their version of Facebook. "Did you hear about Nancy's hip replacement?" Check the bulletin board. "Need a casserole for tomorrow night?" Post it on the bulletin board.

One afternoon, I was headed to the classroom where I taught Sunday school when I noticed a long piece of paper pinned right to the middle of the board. It was unfurled down to the floor, so I decided to check it out—and that's when I read the letter.

To the members of Penn Yan UMC,

Our pastor is praising the sodomites and he is wrong. He thinks he can go against the Bible, but he can't. Leviticus 18:22 says, "A man shall not lie with a man as with a woman, for such is an abomination." There are no excuses for the homosexuals, and our church can't go against the Bible. . . . We can love the sinner, but we can't accept their sin and say it's alright for them to be in our church.

I could feel my face turning red as I skimmed through it. My hands got hot and I began to sweat. I ran home and I could feel the adrenaline rushing through my body. My heart was beating faster than I could think, but I knew what I had to do. I began to type:

> First of all, Sir or Madam who has authored this letter, your name is not evident and so I am unable to address you by name. I find it interesting that you had not admitted to authoring this letter. God knows who you are and knows your thoughts, so you mustn't be hiding from Him. Are you then hiding from your more open-minded Christian sisters and brethren who believe that love and acceptance is the way of the Church? If that be the case, state your views clearly because we are all entitled to opinions. I do implore you, Sir or Madam, to own your words if you are to say them, and not cower behind the guise of a nameless paper. There are several misconceptions in your letter that I would like to counsel you through.

I was seventeen and heavily influenced by reading *The Scarlet Letter* in school. Maybe I got a little carried away, but something inside me caught fire, and it hasn't gone out. Up went my response on the bulletin board—and I signed my name with one of those fat Sharpies just to prove my point. At the time, I was writing the letter because I knew something was wrong. Even though I was still unsure about the whole "gay" thing, I knew in my heart that God couldn't hate people for being who they were. That couldn't be who God is. What I didn't know was that somewhere deep down, I was writing this letter for myself. I think some part of me was trying to say, "See, it's OK to be you." I had grown up learning that "God is love," but this letter made me wonder: *Is God really love*? And if God is love, how could God not love these people too?

So, I decided to study the verses that the unnamed author used in the letter along with other "anti-gay" rhetoric that some Christians use. During my undergraduate studies, I spent a year at Oxford University in England. If I was going to prove those exclusionary Christians wrong, I wanted to be absolutely sure I was right—and where better to do that than Oxford? I was there on a mission to learn and to bring back what I learned. While I was there, I studied Biblical Hebrew, Early Church History (90–500 CE), and Human Sexuality in Ancient Greece and Rome. I sat one-on-one with Oxford professors (called tutors) for a full academic year. I knew that the first tool in disassembling what that person had written in the letter was a study of Scripture and its context, so that's what I set out to do.

GETTING DOWN TO BUSINESS

That anonymous letter used several verses to condemn people who love other people of the same gender. And even as I wrote the above sentence, I could hear the Southern accent of my former campus minister saying, "We don't condemn your love of another man, we just know that if you *act* on that love, it's against God's will." In her mind, she was called to be celibate until marriage, so why shouldn't I be expected to be celibate my whole life? This is how we both obeyed God "equally." It's a thin veil exclusionary

Christians wear—they wouldn't even agree with me calling them "exclusionary." They'd say that they welcome all people (which isn't exactly a lie), but once you're in, you have to be like them or you're out. You have to be a *repentant sinner*, someone who knows they were wrong and says they'll be better. Sure, they're welcoming, but only if you change. That's why I won't use the terms *conservative*, *biblical*, or *traditionalist* to define them—because I've seen biblical inclusive churches whose style is very traditional and there are even some politically conservative folks in these spaces. The Christians I'm talking about are the ones who use the Bible to exclude, so from here on out, they're *exclusionary Christians*. The first reference that most of them cite is Sodom and Gomorrah.

After some sleuthing through Columbia University's library, I found a little old book called *The Book of Gomorrah*. It was written by a Benedictine monk named Peter Damian in 1049 CE. The reason this angsty little book is important is because it's the first time the word *sodomy* is ever used. He just made it up. He added a Greek ending to the name Sodom and, voilà, *sodomia* (sodomy). So just to be clear, *sodomy* wasn't even a word until more than nine hundred years *after* the Bible was compiled. Even the pope at the time (Leo IX) brushed Damian off and told him to mind his own business (that's my paraphrasing anyway). Let's say that sodomy means sexual relations between two men. If this word didn't come into being until 1049, then *sodomite,* which is how we'd describe someone who engaged in sodomy, wasn't a word either. So, those Christians who point to their Bibles and say, "See, sodomy is in here!" are just plain wrong. But it's not entirely their fault—we've all been spoon-fed mistranslations since birth.

It doesn't help matters that many Christian publishers and editors have allowed these mistranslations to continue. That's why it's important to see them publishing books like this for people like us. If we're going to tear down centuries of lies, we need their help too. It's time we religious rejects in all industries say what's really in the "Old Law" (the Torah, as my Jewish friends call it), and see what Paul (and people who used Paul's name) really wrote in the New Testament.

SODOM AND GOMORRAH

For centuries, mistranslations and misinformation have fueled the Church's case against us. The story of Sodom and Gomorrah in Genesis chapter 19 has become the archetype for explaining what God does to gays. For hundreds of years, this story has been used as evidence that God hates the "sodomites," or "homosexuals," or "gays." But we know that *sodomy* was not a word at the time this story was written, and the Bible itself tells us what's wrong with Sodom. Like I pointed out in the last chapter, Ezekiel 16:49 says that the sins of Sodom were "pride, excess of food, and prosperous ease," and they "did not aid the poor and needy." Did you catch that? Sodom was condemned *not* because there were folks in loving same-sex relationships, and also *not* because there were guys who wanted everyone to have gay sexual relationships. Sodom and Gomorrah were condemned—the Bible tells us—because of their pride, their gluttony, and their apathy toward the needy.

Even Jerome (347–420 CE), who was one of the leading theologians in the early Church, said that the sins of Sodom were arrogance and lavish lifestyles.[1] One of the things that made Jerome the "real deal" is that he translated the entire Bible into Latin (it's called the *Vulgate*). He wasn't just good; he was one of the best. In Church terms, we call him one of the "Doctors of the Church" or "Church Fathers." This guy shaped the Church we know today, and when he read the story of Sodom and Gomorrah he *didn't say it condemned gay people*. That's huge. It can be frustrating to think that somehow we're further behind today than fourth-century Christians—but I'm not giving up, and I hope you won't either. What about the other Church Doctors, what did they have to say? Some folks who are even bigger Church nerds than I am might argue that Augustine (354–430 CE) condemned Sodom for its homosexual activity. Well, let's see about that.

One afternoon, I was reading through Augustine's *City of God*. It was an old 1950s English translation that said, "Lot was delivered from Sodom . . . where custom had made *sodomy* as prevalent as laws have elsewhere made other kinds of wickedness."[2] I hope your internal alarm went off. The word *sodomy* isn't in Augustine's Latin, it's a mistranslation in English. Because of translations like this one, lots of exclusionary theologians say that Augustine, and therefore the early Church, condemned the act of sodomy. But here's the problem: Augustine was writing in the fifth century, and as we already observed, *sodomy* wasn't even a word until the middle of the eleventh century. How could Augustine have used a word that didn't exist? The fact is, he didn't. In Latin, the word he used was *stupra*, which comes from the root *stuprum*, meaning "dishonor" or "shame." Just before this indictment, Augustine argued that although there were multiple angels communicating the message of destruction, both Abraham and Lot "recognized the Lord, addressing Him in the singular number."[3] To Augustine, the story of Sodom and Gomorrah was really about believers accepting Jesus and showing hospitality. A lack of hospitality, to Augustine, would cause shame. Somehow over the course of history, the translators decided that shame meant sex, and sex meant sodomy, and sodomy meant all homosexuals deserved to die. They weren't just sloppy, they were wrong.

Another translation I read was even worse; it said that Sodom was a place where "homosexual practices among the males" became common.[4] This translation puts a nineteenth-century idea (homosexuality) into the words of Augustine, a fifth-century theologian. By now I hope you can see how these choices by people at the top—theologians, translators, and publishers—have created a cloud of misinformation that covers the rest of us. So, we're taking on the top, and we're bringing it down in order to raise the rest of Christian believers. And we're doing it together. We're not throwing out the Bible, we're reclaiming it.

LEVITICUS

You shall not lie with a male as with a woman;
it is an abomination.

Leviticus 18:22

If a man lies with a male as with a woman, both of
them have committed an abomination; they shall be
put to death; their blood is upon them.

Leviticus 20:13

We're about to get even more nerdy. You ready? The author of that letter on the bulletin board specifically used Leviticus 18:22 as "proof" that being gay was against the will of God. The Hebrew word *toevah* is translated into English as "abomination" in this verse and in Leviticus 20:13. In the Greek version of the Old Testament (the Septuagint), they used the word *bdelugma*, which means *ritual uncleanness,* and usually refers to idol worship. In the King James Version of the Bible (KJV), there are fifty-nine places where the worship of other gods is called an "abomination." How could these two verses be the exception? The point is, in both biblical languages the sin in Leviticus is an act connected to idol worship—not a type of person who is inherently evil. The verses before and after Leviticus 18:22 refer to acts of idol worship as well. Leviticus 18:21 says, "You shall not give any of your offspring to sacrifice them to Molech [a rival god], and so profane the name of your God." The verse comes right after the supposedly "anti-gay" verse, and it prohibits sex with animals. So, what were all of these "do nots" doing next to each other? What do they have in common?

Remember that word *abomination*? Remember how it's almost always about idol worship? Well, here's the thing: when the people worshipped Molech, they worshipped a statue that looked like a bull with a man's head and shoulders. It was part man, part animal. It's not just a coincidence that these three verses are right next to each other. Don't sacrifice your kids to Molech (v. 21), don't lie with a man as with a woman (v. 22), don't have sex with animals (v. 23). All of these are "abominations," forms of idol worship. Why would the Bible suddenly go from idol worship to a random note about who to love and be in a relationship with and then back to idol worship? It doesn't. They're all about acts related to the worship of Molech, the half man/half animal.

But if this still doesn't tear away the decades of harm we've associated with these verses, here's another detail that is often overlooked. Whatever the crime, in order to bring justice (for the Lord is just), there had to be *two or three* male witnesses (Deuteronomy 19:15). This was the requirement for conviction in the Old Testament. As misogynistic as this was, think about what it means—especially for Leviticus 18:22. Would there ever be two or three other male witnesses to a sexual act? Would the act be something private, like a same-sex couple quietly enjoying each other's company at home? Or, would it have been something public, like the worship of a half man/half animal god, one like Molech?

For a long time, though, I didn't read the verses that came before or after the "anti-gay" verses either. Like many exclusionary Christians, I too was spoon-fed what to believe by people I trusted. And many of us thought they were right—and some folks still do. So, I don't condemn exclusionary Christians, because I understand that overturning everything we were ever taught is difficult—but this doesn't mean they get a lifetime pass to discriminate. Many people haven't had to question these verses before; they may have felt no need to challenge what their pastors and parents and grandparents said. I know it's a journey, and I want us to bring them along into that dream Church too. So, our job is to help others gradually question these verses and deconstruct the harmful interpretations that were passed down to them as the inerrant Word of God.

Only two verses in the King James Version of the Old Testament use the word *sodomite*, Deuteronomy 23:17 and 1 Kings 14:24. These are both mistranslations of *qadesh*, the Hebrew word for "temple prostitute." Not only do both the Hebrew and Greek words for "abomination" refer to idol worship, and not only was the word *sodomy* coined more than nine hundred years after the Bible was completed, but also the word *sodomite* has been haphazardly used by translators to replace the Hebrew word for temple prostitute in the King James Version. This is a huge deal. Essentially, the translators chose to replace temple prostitution with same-sex intercourse, and because of their choice they've condemned us for a crime that was never ours to begin with. Being gay has nothing to do with temple prostitution, but pretending that the crime was sodomy rather than temple prostitution sure helps the exclusionary Christians' argument. So, the Old Testament says nothing about gay people, homosexuality, or even sex between two people of the same sex—unless it's in the form of idol worship.

There are beams in every wall that give the wall shape but aren't necessary to hold up the rest of the house. These beams can be carefully taken out, and the wall can be deconstructed so that the house is more open. In Christianity, we believe that "Christ is the end of the law" (Romans 10:4). Most of us accept that the laws of the Old Testament don't apply to us anymore—it's what Jesus came to free us from. These restrictions are like those beams that can be carefully dismantled. They gave the walls shape, and they help us to understand why Jesus is necessary, but we've moved beyond them and it's time to set them aside. If we truly believe in what the New Testament says about the Messiah, there's no reason to even debate the old laws. We wear blended clothing (outlawed in Leviticus 19:19), and those of us who aren't vegetarian eat all the pork (outlawed in Leviticus 11:7) and shellfish (outlawed in Leviticus 11:10) that we want. These acts are all against the laws in the Torah and carry the same weight as Leviticus 18:22, and yet we've decided these are OK. In Christian theology, we believe that Jesus fulfilled the old laws, and that we're no longer accountable to them—at least most of them. However, this becomes sloppy when people decide that maybe they want to keep one or two of those old laws, and maybe that should be the "anti-gay" one.

Let's take it a step further. How many of us have ever disrespected our parents? According to the Bible, we should be put "to death" (Deuteronomy 21:21). Do you see what's happening? If those same people who use the Old Testament against us were to hold themselves as accountable to each law as they hold us to this one, I bet they'd see things differently. They would experience their faith being used to condemn them rather than liberate them—and that's not what Jesus came to do. So, if the old law doesn't really apply to us anymore (though most folks think the Ten Commandments are worth keeping), then the next place we have to look is the New Testament.

THE NEW TESTAMENT

Do you not know that wrongdoers will not inherit the kingdom of God? Do not be deceived! Fornicators, idolaters, adulterers, male prostitutes, sodomites.

1 Corinthians 6:9

. . . fornicators, sodomites, slave traders, liars,
perjurers, and whatever else is contrary to the
sound teaching.

1 Timothy 1:10

In both 1 Corinthians 6:9 and 1 Timothy 1:10, the Greek word *arsenokoitai* has been translated as "sodomite" in the New Revised Standard Version (NRSV) and several other versions. The New Living Translation is even worse. It translates this word as a condemnation of people "who practice homosexuality." The word *homosexual* didn't enter the English language until the nineteenth century. Most scholars agree that neither the ancient Hebrew people nor the Romans knew what it meant to identify as gay. An identity means that being homosexual is part of how we define ourselves, how we exist in society. To most of the Romans, it was about the position, not the partner. It was perfectly normal to have sex with your male slave as long as you were on top. They didn't understand what it meant to be homosexual because it wasn't about the "object" of their desire, it was about having power over them (regardless of the sex). So, they weren't gay, but they weren't straight either. We have to change the way we think about the ancient world.

Back to 1 Corinthians and 1 Timothy. The author is describing a particular type of activity between men, but what? The Greek word that has been translated as "sodomite" or "homosexual" is *arsenokoitai*, and it's the first time this word is ever used in the New Testament. It's possible that like the word *sodomy*, the author just made it up. The word is a mashup of the Greek words for "male" and "bed." Just like in Leviticus, the context is key. In these verses, *arsenokoitai* is right between male prostitutes and thieves. It's no coincidence that this word falls in a list of sins that are exploitative and transactional. The author is talking about a specific sexual activity that exploits one of the partners and is connected to money. These verses don't say anything about being gay. It's not about the type of person, it's about the act they perform. What the author does say is that the Roman way of penetrating whoever they liked, without regard to the person's own feelings, was wrong. To enslave someone sexually or to prove one's strength or manliness by penetrating an opponent was contrary to how a Christ-follower should behave. Christ came to lower the mountains and raise the valleys, to be the great equalizer, to topple kings, and to lift up the lowly. Proving oneself through rape was not in line with Jesus's teachings of equality, love, and justice.

We know that the word *sodomite* doesn't belong here either. We'd have to wait another nine hundred years for that to come along. So, if *sodomy* wasn't a word, then how could *sodomite*, someone who practiced sodomy, be a word? It wasn't. The word is *arsenokoitai*. The author says nothing about a same-sex relationship that is committed, loving, and affirming of each other's humanity. What the author is condemning is a sexual act in which one partner is exploited. One pastor read this section and then asked, "Is heterosexuality a sin?" Her point was that there's not one answer—it varies by couple. Is one partner abusing the other? If yes, their expression of heterosexuality is sinful. Are the partners respectful and loving of each other? If yes, their expression of heterosexuality is not sinful. It's the same basis for all different types of partners. If the people in the relationship are affirming of each other's humanity and are loving, then their relationship glorifies God. It's not about the sex of the partners, it's about the type of relationship they have.

NATURAL AND UNNATURAL

For this reason God gave them up to degrading passions. Their women exchanged natural intercourse for unnatural, and in the same way also the men, giving up natural intercourse with women, were consumed with passion for one another. Men committed shameless acts with men and received in their own persons the due penalty for their error.

Romans 1:26-27

This passage from Romans is probably the most difficult to understand. It seems pretty clear-cut. Not only does Paul talk about men, he also talks about women exchanging "natural relations for unnatural ones." But what did Paul mean by natural and unnatural? Because I heard the arguments of exclusionary Christians as I grew up, my mind instantly concludes that "natural" means heterosexual relationships, and "unnatural" means homosexual relationships. Is that actually what the verse says? Let's take a look at the context. Right before these verses, Paul is talking about the sin of idolatry. In Romans 1:23, Paul wrote that, "they exchanged the glory of the immortal God for images resembling a mortal human being or birds or four-footed animals or reptiles." Just like Leviticus, Paul is writing about acts of idolatry. The people gave up their worship of God and exchanged it with a worship of other gods that looked like people and animals.

In Romans 1:25, Paul says that the idolaters are without excuse, "because they exchanged the truth about God for a lie and worshiped and served the creature rather than the Creator." Again, it's about acts of idolatry. They knew God but chose to exchange their knowledge and turn away. It's also important to point out that the Christian cults were weird to the Romans. The Christians gathered together, men and women, said that they loved one another, and talked about eating human flesh and drinking human blood. The suspicion of cannibalism aside, it was the fact that men and women gathered together in secret that really made the Romans nervous. Most Roman cults separated men and women. It was OK for a man to penetrate whomever he wanted, but they didn't want to chance that women might enjoy someone else's company too. So, they kept the men and women separate. In 186 BCE, the Roman Senate tried to ban the Dionysian religion because it was an exclusively female cult that, like the male cults, worshipped a god through *orgia*, group sex.

So, some of the pagan cults were places where women who were married to men, and men who were married to women, would go off and exchange their marital vows for a good time of idol worship, sometimes through group sex. Since Paul was talking about idolaters, he was talking about these people and these acts of idol worship. It's just like in Leviticus. The author is condemning the sexual acts of cults that worshipped other gods. This makes sense, and it seems like a much more accurate reading than "Paul hated the gays." Paul did not say that all same-sex couples who were committed Christians should burn in hell. Paul did not condemn same-sex relationships.

Paul condemned acts of idol worship. He condemned married men and women who broke their vows and exchanged their natural knowledge of God with idolatry and joined in the pagan cults. In the all-male and all-female cults, men and women committed "shameless acts" with other men and women—they worshipped other gods together through sex. They knew God but exchanged Her for an idol. They had husbands and wives but exchanged them for group sex in idol worship. This might have been OK for Roman pagans (for the men anyway), but for Christians, sex was deeply connected to the institution of marriage—it became a Christian value. Paul is condemning folks who exchanged their Christian values for pagan ones.

MAGIC?

Even though I'm the one who's studying to be a pastor, my younger brother is probably the most "religious" in our family. In between all-nighters for his computer engineering classes, he leads several Bible studies, prays with people on campus, and goes to worship services that last hours. He's deeply committed to living a biblical life, which I admire. As most campus ministries are, the ones on his campus are mainly in the exclusionary camp. When he found his deeper biblical faith, something began to cause him tension. He was on board with most of their literal interpretations of the Bible because that's how we grew up, but when they talked about homosexuality he was conflicted.

When he was applying to colleges, I had helped him edit his essays. I remember that he didn't want to show me one of them because he was embarrassed. Finally, after I'd nagged him for a bit, he showed me. He wrote about how restrained I was in high school because I didn't seem to fit in and how free I was after I came out as gay in college. He said that he was proud of my confidence in who I really was. He went to college knowing that I was more myself when I was finally able to come out as gay, and yet campus ministries and churches were teaching him that I shouldn't be who I am.

He couldn't accept their condemnation without understanding the foundation of their argument. So, every time we had a break from college, we would stay up for hours talking about biblical interpretations and theology. One night in March 2019, right after I stood up at the General Conference and poured my heart out, we had another conversation. We were sitting down to dinner with almost our entire family, and they knew what would happen. We spent two hours talking, barely noticing when everyone else got up to leave. (Our family thinks that we fight about it, but we've actually found a loving way to have real conversations—and even to disagree sometimes.)

Faith is confusing, and neither of us claims to have the right answers. On that night, while our family was getting up to leave dinner, he said to me, "I saw your speech and I prayed to God, 'Lord, let me hear the cries of your children.' And I finally heard it." He looked at me and continued, "I grew up watching you lead youth group and seeing your passion for God, so it just didn't make sense to me that you could be doing anything other than trying to please God." Even though the churches and groups around him read the English versions of the Bible literally, he was conflicted because they said people like me were intentionally disobeying God's will.

He and I have talked about most of what is in this chapter, though I hope he's surprised by some of the newer research I've added in. After one of our recent conversations he asked me, "Do you think most other Christians actually hate you, or are they just deeply convicted by their beliefs? Would teaching them this stuff change their minds?" I paused and said back to him, "I think it depends on who's teaching them. It has to be someone they trust—otherwise it seems like magic."

I even feel this way sometimes. It seems like it's just too simple. How could these top scholars and Church leaders like my own bishop be so misinformed? How could it be that just by reading a few verses before and after, by looking at the Greek and Hebrew, and by looking at the cultures of the day, we can come to a completely different conclusion than the one the Church has held for hundreds of years? It seems too simple. It seems like magic—but it's not. It's dedicated hours of scholarship. Many, many people came before our generation and did the hard work of noticing these mistranslations and anachronisms. The problem is, much of their work still remains up at the top, in Ivy League schools and seminaries, and the rest of the world doesn't see it. It's time for that to change. You've got the first tool now; you know how to take apart the mess that's been plastered over the beams of Scripture and expose the truth that has always been beneath.

Notes

1. Mark D. Jordan, *The Invention of Sodomy in Christian Theology* (Chicago: University of Chicago Press, 1997), 33.
2. Augustine, *City of God*, trans. Marcus Dods (New York: Random House, 1950), book XVI, chap. 30.
3. Augustine, *City of God*, book XVI, chap. 29.
4. Augustine, *City of God*, trans. Eva Sanford and William Green (Cambridge, MA: Harvard University Press, 1965).

Chapter 3

BORN THIS WAY

What was your favorite Halloween costume? When I was five years old, my mom spent weeks in a little room making me a surprise costume. I wasn't allowed to peek in or see anything at all until Halloween night. On that special and spooky evening, she emerged from the mysterious room of creation and strapped two giant metal wings onto my arms. OK, they weren't really metal, but they were the coolest tinfoil-wrapped pieces of cardboard I'd ever seen. On that night, my dreams of being "J. J. the Jet Plane" (like the old cartoon) came true. I was ready to run outside and show my friends, but something happened as I ran to the door. Just as I started to walk through the doorway my wings clunked against the sides—I didn't fit. My costume was too big! I had to turn sideways and squeeze my way through.

Even though my mom worked hard to make my costume, it didn't quite fit and made it more difficult for me to go where I wanted. Sure, I still got to trick-or-treat, but it took me a while to get around—and I took up the entire sidewalk. For those of us in the LGBTQ+ community, our lives can feel like we're wearing an awkward airplane costume. Sometimes, our families, church communities, and school friends even construct costumes for us. They have a certain image of who they hope we'll become, and sometimes we start to internalize their expectations and strap on their costume ourselves.

When I joined the school musical in middle school, I was worried that my family and friends would suspect I was gay. Theater wasn't something the other boys did. When I sang "Summer Nights" from *Grease* in Sandy's octave instead of in the "man's octave," I was worried that my costume of being a "normal" boy would tear a bit. I was preoccupied with maintaining my costume of straightness. I didn't want others to question who I was—and I definitely wasn't ready to face myself. It was a terrifying and exhausting time. Looking back, I can't help but wonder: if I had taken off the costume—if I had stopped trying to act how everyone thought I should—how much happier would my middle school and high school years have been? Or, better yet, what if someone else had helped me to recognize the real me hiding under the costume of straightness? What if my church had openly said there wasn't just one normal type of love in God's eyes? What if my sex education class talked about safety in more than just heterosexual relationships? What if the school board had made our district a safe space for people like me to discover ourselves?

Some of us aren't ready to tear the costume, and like middle school me, some of us might not even know we're wearing one. To live your entire life seeing only heterosexual couples on the sidewalks, seeing only heterosexual couples in movies and on television, being asked only if you had a crush on someone of the opposite gender, and having your church never speak about homosexuality at all—it creates a certain kind of normal; and if your love doesn't match the normal, it feels wrong. I didn't just feel different, I felt wrong. The work of discovering who we are is difficult, especially when the world around us seems to forget we exist—or outright tells us we're unworthy. As we explore our own identities—the ones that might be in tension with movies, families, and churches—we have to be able to see beyond the world that's presented to us. We can't accept the heterosexual white love stories or the male-only occupations as normal.

Just like we did earlier with the Bible, we have to question and deconstruct the norms that have been passed down and pushed upon us. It shouldn't be normal to live in a world where people are discriminated against, abused, and cast aside because they have been created differently than the straight white men who define normal for us. We have to question everything we've been told about what is normal and rediscover the world for ourselves—rediscover *ourselves* for ourselves. This is how we go about liberation—by breaking the chains we might not even know hold us captive. We must question, and then we can begin to reclaim the beauty of our God-given identities and our place in the churches and institutions we hold dear.

IT'S A JOURNEY

As I think about the costumes that the world forces upon us—sometimes with good intentions—it reminds me of the story of Jacob and Esau in Genesis 27. Jacob's father, Isaac, was old and was about to pass away. Jacob was the younger brother, so most of what his father owned would go to his older brother, Esau. Rebekah, the boys' mother, tried to make sure that Jacob was taken care of. She cooked up Isaac's favorite meal and told Jacob to bring it to his father—but he had to dress as his older brother Esau. Esau was a hairy man, so Jacob put some goat hair on his arms and brought the food to his blind father. "Father, it's me, Esau," Jacob said, "Give me your blessing" (Genesis 27:19, paraphrased). Isaac reached out and felt Jacob's arms. "You feel like Esau," he said, "but you sound like Jacob. Is it really you, Esau?" Jacob said, "Yes, it's me, Esau" (Genesis 27:22-24, paraphrased) and he went away with his brother's inheritance and his father's blessing.

Even though Jacob's mother might have meant well, she encouraged her son to hide his true self in order to get ahead. I won't criticize Rebekah because she's one of the few powerful biblical women we have. Thanks to Rebekah, we can say that women were never as passive as many exclusive Christians would like them to be. Instead, what I see in this story is a mother who cares and who is aware that the rules of her society are unfairly stacked against her son. So, as any well-intentioned mother would, she did what she could to ensure his success. When I first came out, my mom was apprehensive. She loved me and she didn't want others in our small town to be critical. If I made a joke about my sexuality in front of our church friends, she would give me a look like, "Did you really just say that?" I think she was worried what cruel things others might say. Maybe my mom, like Rebekah, was trying to do what she could within our society to help me live the best life I could. My mom and I have come a long way on the journey of understanding, and she comes to almost all of my sermons wearing a name tag that proudly says, "J. J.'s Mom" (it's really cute).

A few chapters later in Jacob's story, we learn that he became quite successful, but he wanted to return to his homeland. So, he sent some messengers to his brother Esau, and Esau told them that he'd meet Jacob in the morning. Jacob was terrified, and that night, he went out to a river where he was met by a strange being. Jacob and the being wrestled all night long (though we're not really sure why they were wrestling in the first place). Jacob was winning, even though the being knocked his hip out of place. Daybreak was approaching and for some reason the being had to leave. Jacob said, "I'll let you go—but first you have to bless me" (Genesis 32:26, paraphrased). So, the being asked him, "What's your name?" Jacob responded, "Jacob." The being said back, "Not anymore. You've wrestled with God and with people and you've overcome them both. You will now be called Israel, which means 'the one who strives or wrestles with God'" (Genesis 32:27-28, paraphrased).

In order to receive his father's blessing, Jacob had to cover up who he really was—it may have seemed like the only way to be successful. When Jacob was wrestling with that being (a god? an angel? a man? we can't say for sure), he still had a deep desire to be blessed—to be accepted and affirmed by a being whom he believed to be God. I don't know about you, but even though I'm confident in my sexuality, it feels good to hear a pastor or religious person affirm it. It's nice to be blessed for who we are. This time, when Jacob asked to be blessed, he used his own name. When he approached God by the river, he was blessed for who he was—not who he pretended to be. Jacob no longer had to hide his true identity to gain approval; he was worthy just as he was.

If we're still questioning everything, then do we really believe that a human could beat God in a wrestling match? Perhaps the writers of this strange story weren't really talking about wrestling. Jacob was somehow able to beat God, but this epic battle didn't end with a big championship belt; it ended with Jacob's ability to be himself. It's as though the writers were saying, "Be yourself, because that's the greatest strength you have." That may sound like the *Veggie Tales* version, but this story shows us that we don't have to hide any longer; it invites us out of the closets and secret web browsers, and into the fullness of who we are. Somehow, in the course of a few chapters, Jacob gained the confidence to be himself, and he was blessed because of it.

The reason I like Jacob's story so much is because

he didn't come to terms with himself overnight. Jacob deceived his family, was aided by a well-meaning and confident woman, hid who he was, and ran far away. Eventually, Jacob gained the courage to face God and his family as his true self, and we can too. But, like Jacob, this self-acceptance is a journey. Maybe you're right in the middle of it as you read this. The Bible is full of stories where people disguised themselves and hid who they were. So, we're in good company.

Once Adam and Eve realized that they were naked, they tried to hide behind trees. They didn't think that their true and naked selves were worthy of God's love. Moses's identity was hidden for his protection (he was the wrong nationality). Sarah was asked by Abraham to hide her identity when they traveled through Egypt (apparently, her looks were too tempting). In all of these stories, the heroes or heroines tried to cover up who they truly were because they feared what others might think or do to them. But, in all of these stories, God was most pleased—and the protagonists were happiest—when they were able to embrace who they really were and share their true selves with the world.

Adam and Eve were in a close relationship with God before they hid behind the trees—God already knew their naked truths before they did. When Moses figured out his true identity, seas were parted, an oppressed people was set free, and new books about God were added to the Torah. Sarah and Abraham went on to found a new nation, and

Jacob became the father of many. All of these biblical heroes and heroines became great when they accepted themselves and cast aside the costumes—both the ones that others put on them, and the ones they didn't know they were wearing.

Many of us are in places where churches or governments continue to force LGBTQ+ folks to wear costumes that hide our queerness. For some, the time has not yet come when you feel safe enough to shred your costume. If you can't get rid of it in public, maybe you're able to shred it for yourself—to embrace yourself as the beautiful person you truly are. Whether it's in front of others or alone in front of the mirror, when we allow ourselves to be who we've always been deep down, we allow God to work in new ways. We not only allow ourselves to experience God but also enable others to experience God through the *true* versions of us. The journey to self-acceptance can be long— and even dangerous—but we don't have to face it alone. We're a global community of queer kids and allies, and we can be there for one another. We can reclaim religious spaces and biblical stories together and show the world a new way to see God. This all starts with our ability to see ourselves as good and claim our true names as legitimate.

VERY GOOD

It was mid-August and I was preaching at a church in central California. After the service, as I was sweating in my pink sport coat and shaking hands, an older man pulled me aside. We sat down in the entryway as everyone else went on to get some rainbow cake in the reception hall. He looked at me with a big smile and said, "You're so brave." I said, "Thank you, but it was you and your generation that made this possible." He kept smiling and said, "You know, when I was your age, I didn't want to be gay. I went to the Mormon Church and asked them to help me. I went through conversion therapy for three years . . . but it didn't work."

He chuckled and then said, "They asked if I wanted to be excommunicated, and I told them that it was their choice. I tried everything they told me, but I couldn't change. When the war started in Vietnam I was drafted, and I secretly hoped that something would happen to me over there. If my life was taken in the war, then at least I wouldn't bring my family shame for being gay." He paused and look down at the carpet as the sun stretched our shadows toward the sanctuary. "I tried to commit suicide several times because no one could fix me and make me straight. I turned to drugs and alcohol and then to Christian Science. I joined a twelve-step program and that's when I found this church. I felt a fuzziness come over me, and for the first time I realized that I was good. I felt like God could love me and that I could one day love myself."

When God looked out over all of creation in Genesis chapter 1, God said, "It is very good." God didn't say, "Well, the grass is a bit long over here," or "Those people are a bit obnoxious." God didn't critique creation in this story—but God didn't say it was perfect either. *Goodness and perfection are different.* When we mix these two ideas, we start to believe that just because we're imperfect we're not good either. This is a very harmful theological mix-up, so I want you to hear these words: *you* are *very good.* Even the biblical writers, the ones who wrote about an angry and jealous God, agreed that when God looked at the world, She saw its innate goodness. God didn't see perfection, God saw goodness.

As I sat in the entryway of that California church, I witnessed a shimmer in the eyes of an eighty-five-year-old man as he said, "I realized that I was good." Even then, decades after this realization, he was filled with joy to repeat those words. No matter how far down the paths of no return we may have gone, no matter how many times we've royally screwed up, the truth of our faith is that we are and will always be very good in the eyes of God. For many of us, it's difficult to accept this. It's hard to see ourselves as worthy of being loved when our churches and communities and families have told us the opposite, or have driven us to do horrible things. They've drilled into our minds a chasm of imperfection that they claimed we could cross only if we were different. They needlessly created an impossible problem for us and said that Jesus was the answer.

I believe Jesus is the answer to a lot of things, but he didn't come to magically turn queer kids into straight ones. Jesus came to heal, to love, and to liberate—to set the entire world free from the chains that keep us from loving

God, loving our neighbors, and loving ourselves. When we're able to feel the unconditional love of God, we're able to love ourselves more fully, and we're able to love others more abundantly as well. We are very good, and it's time we come out as our fabulous and very good selves—even if it's just in the mirror.

COMING OUT GOOD

During the summer of 2019, I spoke at the first ever United Methodist Queer Pride Camp. It was led by queer clergy, and all who attended were queer Christians between the ages of eighteen and thirty-five. On the second-to-last day, there was a service to remember our baptism. As one of the pastors stirred the waters, she began to tear up and said, "You are wanted here. These waters are for all of us. We don't have to hide or feel dirty any longer. You are loved and you are wanted."

As we all came forward, some of the campers were overcome with emotion. Some let their tears stream into the bowl as they washed their foreheads with the baptismal waters. One girl who was about nineteen years old came up to me in tears and said, "I've never felt like I was truly welcomed in a church. I've always had to hide part of me, and I've never felt safe in a church before." For many of us, this remembrance meant revisiting those dark moments where our own self-loathing told us we didn't matter, where our churches and families rejected us and made us feel unclean. We remembered the darkness, but in that space of queer Christians, we experienced the light of coming out good. For some of them, this was the first time that they realized they could come out as somewhere on the LGBTQ+ spectrum *and* see themselves as wonderfully made, beautifully good images of God.

Like I said before, I didn't have gay role models to look up to when I was growing up. In my town, you were either normal (straight) or you were wrong (anyone else). When I got to college, I was exposed to a brave new world. I didn't know this at the time (so it was probably a God thing), but Sarah Lawrence College is the most LGBTQ+ friendly campus in the US. Though my former campus minister would like to believe that the college made me gay, when I stepped foot on the beautiful green grounds for the first time, I experienced a place where people were comfortable being their true selves. It was a place where discovering ourselves was encouraged—even if that meant dyeing our hair a few different colors before we found the right one or using different pronouns as the years went by. Sarah Lawrence was, perhaps for the first time, the place where I experienced what it felt like to be me.

In the stone classroom of my first poetry class, I was given the ability to express my newly unearthed self, to wrestle with the most difficult challenge of all: self-acceptance. As the year went on, I wrote a poem called "Shout," which was inspired by an older gay poet named Allen Ginsberg. "My mouth sips wine on Sunday—but my body is unsatisfied / and it seeks salvation from tan skin. /

My wooden pulpit of purity is hacked, tattered, and torn to shreds by 'natural' instincts." For so long I thought that coming out as gay meant giving in to sin and temptation. That the perfect Christian boy I had tried to be would be tarnished. I was wrong. For months I struggled, and each time that I began to accept my sexuality I was caught in an internal battle. My small-town Christianity, coupled with an exclusive campus ministry, had conditioned me for so long that I believed a choice had to be made: would I be Christian, or would I be gay?

My faith was essential to me, and yet part of my existence was left uncared for. My sexuality was intentionally neglected so that my faith could be preserved from my "sinful" thoughts. It was a dark time that I've tried to forget. I felt like Jacob, wrestling in the darkness and being struck on the side—having part of me bruised and put out of place. As many of you know, this darkness can last a long time.

As my first semester at Sarah Lawrence ended, I realized that I couldn't wrestle in the dark any longer. I couldn't survive in hiding. It was the end of December 2015, and my friends and I were packing to go home for the holidays. I squished as much as I could into my suitcase and headed down the hill toward the train station. It felt like a Harry Potter movie, as we left the old buildings and the lamps illuminated the falling snow. It's a six-hour train ride from New York City to Syracuse, New York, and then an hour-and-a-half drive to our small town, Penn Yan.

As I sat on the train, the lights of the city faded, and the scenery shifted to big shipping boats on the Hudson River. The ride had become somewhat of a ritual for me, and I memorized the view. After the river come dense forests, and then broken barns and farm fields, which stretch across the hilly landscape. The scenery always reminded me that I was leaving the hustle and bustle—and openness—of the city. I always felt a quiet despair.

The train whistled as it arrived in Syracuse at almost ten p.m. I stepped off the train and struggled down the platform with my overstuffed suitcase. I remember feeling more and more dread filling my body as I got closer to my dad's blue truck. "Hey, buddy!" he said, in his loud and excited voice. "Hey, Dad," I said. We hugged, and he put my suitcase in the back. I like my dad. Sure, he watches Fox News and his voice is always a bit too loud, but he means well. He was lonely after he and my mom divorced, so he'd visit me almost once every month in New York City. We grew closer, maybe out of mutual loneliness, but it was nice. This time, however, I felt like I couldn't hide the one thing I never told him.

"You seem quiet, J. What's up?" he said, as we drove through the thick upstate snow. "Nothing, I'm just tired from college," I said, and then looked out of the window. It felt like the fabric of who he thought I was was about to tear. I couldn't stretch my costume any longer, but I didn't know what it was like to live as my full self around him. What if he didn't accept me?

"Something's bothering you. What's up?" He repeated his question, and my heart began to beat faster. I felt paralyzed. My chest was tight, and my breathing got shallow. I couldn't do anything except look away into the darkness. After a while he said, "You know, J . . ." I looked over but didn't meet his eyes. Then, all of a sudden, he said, "If you're gay, that's OK."

Release. The fear that had manifested in my tense shoulders suddenly, and without warning, eased, and my body relaxed into the seat. I still didn't have the words to respond. I took out my phone and showed him a photo of my first boyfriend and me standing next to a Christmas tree. "You two look good together," he said, and we continued the journey home. Later that same Christmas, I came out to my mom and my five other siblings. I had already come out to my oldest sister at Thanksgiving. It was during that Christmas holiday when I finally began to see the dawn in my years-long late-night struggle of self-acceptance.

WHAT IF?

I realize that I'm one of the lucky ones. Sure, my parents said some pretty homophobic things as I was growing up, but when I came out to them, they were willing to take the journey of understanding sexuality with me. But what if they hadn't been willing? I have shirts that are stained with the tears of queer kids—and adults—whose parents were unwilling to take this journey. Parents, this journey is just as confusing for us as it is for you. We might not have the right words to describe it, and we may have acted straight before—we may even have believed we were—but we're coming to you now as your children. We seek to be ourselves, salvaged from beneath the weight of everything we were told we should be. Release from your hands the dreams of lives you hoped we'd live and love us as we are. Listen to your kids, give them the freedom to explore, and be willing to learn along the way. I don't expect you to have the "right" words either, but be willing to walk the journey.

After I preached at the Queer Pride Camp in California, a person in their twenties came up to me. "Where are you from?" I asked them. "Arizona, but my mom's in Maryland." "Wow, that's quite a distance," I said. "What brought you so far from home?" They looked down, "My mother told me I had a choice: be queer or live in her house. We both know it's not a choice," they said, looking up to meet my eyes. "So I packed up my car and drove to Arizona to live with my aunt." Their circumstance was the one I feared so many years ago. They're living my long-feared *what if* scenario.

Everyone's experience is different, and some of us just get lucky. But their mother's rejection wasn't the end of their story. They made their way to Arizona, found someone they loved, and are happily married to a trans man. They are active in their local church, which celebrates their queerness and helped to pay their way to be at the queer camp. Even though their mother hasn't come around, they found a church and a partner that support them and affirm their inherent goodness.

There's no darkness as terrifying as the darkness of self-hatred. What if your church doesn't accept you? What if your friends don't understand? What if your closest friend realizes that you're different? What if your family rejects you? Maybe you've wondered these questions hundreds of times, terrified by the thought that who you are might not be accepted by the people you care about. When these questions storm our minds, wc can rcturn to the truth that we are very good. No matter what our families, churches, or friends threaten to do to us, we can have confidence in the truth that we have been wonderfully made, that we are very good, and that we are called beautifully beloved by God.

In the midst of all your *what ifs*, I hope you can cast aside the one that asks, "What if I have to choose between my faith and my sexuality?" I hope you can begin to silence the voice that questions, "What if I'm not worthy? What if God can't love me?" When the morning light began to shine, Jacob's wrestling match came to end. Even though he had been badly bruised and had been so busy struggling that he didn't have a chance to rest—the dawn came. As the light shone through the clouds, Jacob gained the confidence to speak his true name before God, and he was blessed because of it.

If it hasn't already, the dawn will come in your story. You will be able to be your true self—and you will be blessed because of it. If it's unsafe for you to come out to your family, you have the opportunity to come out to yourself—to love yourself exactly as God created you. When we're finally able to overcome our internal struggle, to look in the mirror and say, "I am very good," we begin to live the new life Jesus talked so much about. As my queer Filipino clergy mentor often says, "Our queerness is a gift." It enables us to explore God and ourselves in new ways. Our queerness puts us in tension with the Church and makes us question what everyone else takes for granted. Your queerness is not a disease or a sin. You have been given a gift, a reason to question and explore God for yourself. It's time we see our queerness as a gift and not as a reason to feel shame. It's time we look in the mirror and confidently say, "We're born this way."

Chapter 4

WE ARE THE CHURCH

When I gather with folks to talk about LGBTQ+ inclusion, I often use the word *queer*. Almost every time I say this, I get a strange look followed by the question, "Is it OK to say (and they whisper) *queer*?" Usually it's an older man who asks, and he's probably been offended by it. After all, it has been used as a slur. Even today, some of us are yelled at by passing cars or whispered about by others on the bus or in the classroom. We're called names by high school bullies or grown-up bigots. Queer. Fag. Butch. Lesbian. Gay. Trans. They've all been used against folks at one time. In high school, if someone called me gay it was the worst insult in the world. Gay was the last thing I wanted to be.

During my first year of college, as I lived in that inclusive environment, something changed for me. For the first time, people didn't use gay as an insult, it was how they identified. It was just part of who they were. I started to embrace it as well. A word that had been my biggest fear and hated insult had become something I felt comfortable identifying with—something I found power in. I chose to reclaim the word *gay* for myself, to take the power away from those who tried to use it for discrimination. Being gay is something I'm proud of. I reclaimed this word that had been used against me, and I embraced it because it's part of who I am.

It took me a few more years to get comfortable with the word *queer*. Gay was bad, but queer seemed more taboo for some reason. I remember sitting on my friend's bed in her dorm room during my sophomore year. She was a senior and one of the only other Christians I knew on campus. She grew up in a conservative area and one of her parents was a pastor. She accepted that I was gay and that many of her friends identified somewhere on the LGBTQ+ spectrum, but it didn't seem like she truly believed it was OK.

The exclusive campus ministry (affiliated with Campus Crusade for Christ, which we later ended) made the leaders sign a covenant, and part of that covenant made us promise that we wouldn't act on same-sex desires. I thought I was the only one, but as we sat on her bed she said, "I haven't told anyone yet, but I'm queer." "What?!" I said, jumping a little on her bed as she smiled. "I've always known I was attracted to more than just men," she said, "but I didn't believe I could actually be this way."

After we hugged (and laughed at how many queer leaders were in our exclusive-minded Christian Union), I asked why she identified with the word *queer*. "The other labels just don't fit me," she said. Queer can mean many things, and it can also act as an umbrella term for

LGBTQ+. Today, queer theory and queer studies have become academic disciplines, and queer theology is an emerging field. In the academy, we've reclaimed the word *queer* as a proper discipline, and not as an insult. For so long, the histories of people who enjoyed romance or sex with others of the same gender, or with others who don't identify with the sex they were born into, have been condemned. Now, queer has become a discipline that seeks to reclaim not only the word but also our histories and our place in the world. It's become something to celebrate and jump on a bed about with your best friend.

But reclaiming a word like *queer* is a process, and we each go through it at our own pace. Just because I'm comfortable using it after years of wrestling with it doesn't mean that you have to be comfortable as well. Just because we give our friends or parents permission to refer to us as queer or gay or lesbian doesn't mean they have permission to call another person that. I use the word *queer*, but if a grandmother who meets me at an event goes home and starts saying queer all the time, she might upset some folks—and not just the exclusive ones. (This has actually happened, bless her heart.) Sometimes we think we're being inclusive, but the words we use are still provoking. It takes time and it takes building relationships before we try to define one another.

The point is that to reclaim a word like *queer*—or *church*—means to take the power away from the oppressor, and this process is personal. Ask before you label. Don't let the bullies define you. Your sexuality is a gift, and if you haven't yet, one day you'll be able to celebrate exactly who you are. As we grow and explore, we begin to reclaim words and identities that others have tried to define for us, and this doesn't only apply to sexuality. One of the most powerful words I think it's time for us to reclaim is *church*, and it starts by exploring what this word really means.

AN ASSEMBLY

I've always loved history. Math and science were never my thing—I just didn't have a passion for numbers— but history is a whole different story. In middle school, I would spend most of my time on my history homework, reading the textbook for hours (and neglecting my math worksheets). I stayed up late to paint a poster of Poseidon or study the long houses of the local indigenous tribes. When I got to Oxford, it was like a nerdy paradise for me. I loved the history of the buildings—how the libraries where I read were hundreds of years older than the United States. It felt like I was living in a museum—but we could actually touch the exhibits.

When the term started, I had tutorials on Early Church History, and it was during those one-on-one meetings every week that my two passions, the Church and history, were brought together. I learned that the word *church* is an English translation of the Greek *ecclesia*, meaning assembly. This word, which has come to mean so much to many people, is simply a translation for a gathering of folks. From these early days, church was understood by the Christ-following Jews and Gentile converts as an assembly of people who sang, joined in a special meal together, and called one another "sister" and "brother." That's what church was, a family gathering. But that's not all it was.

To attend the assemblies of the Christ-followers was inherently political. For much of Rome's history, politics and religion were almost inseparable. The emperor was seen as a god, and even the virtues of the city itself were deified in the goddess Roma. A good Roman attended one of the imperial cults as an act of worship *and* as an act of political obedience. Sure, the Jewish/Christian God might have seemed odd to the first-century Romans—God wasn't part of a pantheon, and God didn't behave like the others or have an image, except in the form of some crucified criminal. Our God was weird to them, but that wasn't the only thing that made the Romans uneasy.

By leaving the Roman cults, the Christ-followers made a political statement. Like the pharaohs of Egypt, the emperors of Rome wanted their people to worship them. After Julius Caesar was assassinated, he became known as *divus Iulius*, the "divine Julius." His adopted son, Octavian (known to most as Augustus), was called *divi filius*, "son of the god." The opening of the Gospel according to Mark, which Church historians believe to be the oldest Gospel, begins unlike the others with this statement: "The beginning of the good news of Jesus Christ, *the Son of God*." Mark's opening seems to be a parody of the emperor's title. The early Christ-followers made it clear that their true King wasn't in Rome—and that made their gatherings political ones.

To attend one their assemblies was seen as an act of defiance. No longer were the citizens worshipping the virtues the empire prided itself on. Maybe the empire feared that the grasp of control it had on its citizens was beginning to loosen. If the citizens weren't worshipping the emperor, where did their allegiance lie? Not only that, but the values of the Christ-following assemblies differed from those of the empire. The Christ-followers weren't concerned with the accumulation of wealth, family status, gender, or even nationality. Of course, not all of the Christ-followers were perfect, and biases did exist, but the assemblies we see in the book of Acts show a good effort at a multicultural communal lifestyle.

In Acts 2, the author writes, "They would sell their possessions and goods and distribute the proceeds to all, as any had need" (Acts 2:45). We are told of communities where individual material wealth was given up so that everyone would be taken care of. We see the temple rejects banding together and showing the world how they believed these Christ-following assemblies of our time should act. These early communities disrupted the status quo, refused to worship a power-hungry nation or leader, and set out to do life differently. They were bold and they were committed to the idea that the creator of the universe loves us dearly. They were committed to a creator who would take on the flesh of a brown refugee, show us how we're supposed to behave, and die and rise again, so that the *world* would be renewed and that we would experience the power of liberation. They were committed to a life-changing and paradigm-shifting message that should continue to challenge our assumptions of who's in and who's out.

The early churches posed a threat to the empire because they refused to worship the emperor, his values, or his gods. In our day, we see Donald Trump retweeting posts hailing him as the second coming of God.[1] Somehow the political family of Christ-following assemblies today, as later happened in Rome, has become synonymous with the empire itself. *Church* has become a trigger word. Sunday worship continues to be the most segregated time in the US, and queer kids are harmed by church folk who won't accept them as they are. Trans people are called the wrong gender or walk into a church that has only two gendered bathroom choices. Maybe the idea of church brings you pain because, as with so many of us, it reminds you of a time, a place, and a people who have harmed you or invalidated who you are, and maybe continue to do so. Even as I attend seminary to serve in the Church, I am continually trying to disassociate it from the harm its people have inflicted. It's hard to reclaim church, but it's time to take the power away from the oppressor and resurrect its true meaning.

NICE CHRISTIANS

During the final leg of my journey to thirty-two churches in the summer of 2019, my partner decided to join me as I was traveling through California for three weeks. He's an atheist and a PhD candidate in theoretical physics who grew up in what was formerly East Germany. Before we met, he never thought he'd find himself in so many churches. Growing up, the Church wasn't an institution he wanted to be a part of, a conviction he still holds. But he came with me as we drove for hours every day to visit churches throughout the state, and he endured the not-so-glamorous life of a traveling gay preacher. Toward the end of our three-week journey we were sitting in a pastor's guest house when my partner said something that shocked me.

It was the night before he was headed back to Canada, and we were sitting on an old red sofa. "You know," he said, smiling a little as he looked over at me, "I've met a lot of nice Christians on this trip." Even now, I smile as I think of him saying this. He had an idea of who Christians were, what we believed, and how we acted. The Church, as an institution, doesn't do a great job of giving us a better reputation. To many people, including my partner, Christians are hypocritical deniers of science whose old book has been used by the alt-right to justify hate crimes against black folks, queer folks, women, immigrants, and people living at the intersections of these identities. And the Church? Well, that's the institution that ordained deadly massacres of believers from other faith traditions. It's the institution that denies us marriage, is still segregated in many places, and serves as the vehicle for neocolonialism (the way countries like the US continue to assert power over other countries).

That *is* the history and continued reality of the Church. Christians are discriminating against folks as you read this page, and the Church as an institution is continuing to discriminate. And yet, those of us who have experienced the mystical power of faith, who have encountered God in some form or another and cannot deny Her presence in our lives, continue to call ourselves Christians and the Church our home. Even though some Christians have inflicted harm upon us, we call ourselves Christians too. *Church* is a word that has been used against us, and yet we too have a right to be here. We are the Church too.

It's our God-given, Jesus-commanded, and Spirit-filled calling to be the Black Lives Matter–campaigning, science-embracing, immigrant- and gay-rights-advocating people whom God has created us to be. The ones who focus less on who and how others should love and more on showing love ourselves. Now, maybe you're like my partner and when you think of the Church, the sins of the institution flood your mind. But my visits to churches across the country have encouraged me because when I think of church, I think of them—the people and places where my atheist partner experienced hospitality, progressive values, and love. I know that the church isn't only a place of harm, and that church people can be more than the exclusive ones might like the world to believe.

Maybe you're more of a cradle Christian like me, and

you've grown up calling the Church your home. Even though your friends can't understand why you possibly stay in this often-corrupt institution, you know there's another side of the story. Maybe you know that we're called to be different, and that Jesus was more like Dr. King and Alexandria Ocasio-Cortez than the neo-Nazis and white supremacists of our time. Maybe you still have a desire deep in your soul to be loved, and you're holding out hope that the Church can offer that to you.

Whoever you are, and whatever your background, we have the opportunity not just to be good people, but to be called Christians and have that mean something powerful, something authentic, and something that provides liberation for all. We—the so-called religious rejects of churches who seek exclusivity and a misinformed understanding of "biblical obedience"—*we* are the church. We are a global assembly who can't stay silent in our closets any longer. It's time we rise up, use our voices, and reclaim the idea of what church is. From now on, church should be a place of liberation and unconditional love for all.

RAINBOW CHALICE

After I gave my speech at General Conference, I walked outside the convention center in St. Louis to get some air. As I was walking around, the news media started showing up to report on the final outcomes. I could imagine the headlines they'd report: "Another denomination denies rights to the LGBTQ+ community." One of the reporters came to me and asked me to give an interview about the ending of the conference with someone from a United Methodist Church in Kenya. His name is Rev. Kennedy Mwita, and I knew that the laws in his country didn't allow marriages between people of the same sex, so I wasn't sure what he would say.

After the interview, Rev. Mwita said that he was deeply saddened by the outcome. He wanted all people to know that they were welcome in our Church, and that his church would continue to be a safe space for LGBTQ+ folks on the continent of Africa. We hugged, and I thanked him for his work and leadership. It was amazing to me that he would risk his career and his life for us.

The next day, we were both asked to speak at a closing worship service for LGBTQ+ folks and allies. He shared his passion and commitment to working together around the world to make safe spaces for LGBTQ+ people. He dreamed of a global church that would work together for justice on all sorts of issues. Together, we have the potential to transform the world. I spoke after him and shared a similar vision, thanking him and our other global allies for their witness. It's powerful to know that queer kids around the world might one day feel comfortable to be themselves—and to think that the Church might actually be on the right side of history.

After the service, an older man with a few white hairs on his head handed me a rainbow communion chalice. "I'm a potter and I make these myself," he said. "I want you to

have this and to continue to make God's table open to all."
I'm such a church nerd, so Communion is very special to
me. Communion, after all, is what a pastor blesses—and it's
only now that queer people (in some places) are allowed to
be pastors and open about our whole selves. I thanked him
and kept greeting folks while smiling and holding my new
rainbow chalice.

I was getting ready to leave when Rev. Mwita came up
to me. He looked down at the rainbow chalice, and then
back up at me. "Where did you get that?" he asked. "I'd love
to take one back to my country and share Communion with
it." I looked around for the potter, but he was gone. I looked
back at Rev. Mwita and then down at the chalice again.

"Here," I said. "Take this one." His eyes shined and he
smiled joyfully. We hugged again and he packed it safely in
his bag. A few weeks later, I received the following email
from him:

> Dear J. J. Warren,
>
> I must say it was a great privilege meeting you during
> my visit to the USA. Despite the unexpected result from the
> Special General Conference 2019 at St. Louis, I believe we still
> have lots to do, to even bond more to build the kingdom of
> God. . . .
>
> It should be known that people who suffer are our
> brothers and sisters, the LGBTQIA+ and their allies in Africa. It
> is my desire that we continue the discussion to empower and
> encourage our friends in Africa who are wrongly victimized
> and oppressed.

No matter how bad it seems, we're not alone—in your hometown or anywhere around the world. There are allies who are risking their lives alongside us to correct the injustices committed against us. We won't have to hide much longer, and Rev. Mwita is part of the reason, as are you. The Church has done us a lot of harm, and yet that pastor and people like him are making safe spaces for LGBTQ+ folks around the world. We're not alone, and he proved that.

A few months ago, it was announced that Rev. Mwita's church, First United Methodist Church of Moheto, Kenya, voted to become a reconciling congregation. Reconciling Ministries Network is a community of more than one thousand United Methodist churches and communities (and some independent churches) that are committed to being safe spaces for LGBTQ+ people. To join the network means that a church has talked with its community about what it means to identify as LGBTQ+, has discussed and learned together about gender identities and gender expression, and is committed to fully supporting LGBTQ+ people in their own church and with others around the world. By the time you read this, his church will officially be the first reconciling church in all of Africa.

That rainbow chalice will always be a powerful memory for me. It's a symbol of our global struggle for understanding and queer inclusion. It represents the turning of tides—that one day the Church will no longer be a place of exclusion, and that Christians will be on the front lines of social progression. While I travel and rally support for this movement, I think of the others who can't be as open as I am. Some of us are forced to live in the shadows because they face persecution and even death.

The reason I can't leave the word *church* behind—the reason I want to reclaim it—is that every time I think about it, I think of that rainbow chalice and the safety that one church offers to queer people in Africa. When I think of church now, pain isn't my primary reaction. Now, the word fills me with hope. I think of that pastor and the queer kids in that community who won't have to live in the shadows. I think of the thousands of people who are committed to justice and inclusion around the world. It's been a long process for me to personally reclaim the word, but I'm glad I have, and they've all been part of that process. Now, it's your turn, and you're not alone in this process either.

A MANIFESTO

Since the last global gathering of my denomination, The United Methodist Church has witnessed something prophetic. Churches in the US have voted out almost all exclusive-minded delegates for the next General Conference in May. Same-sex weddings are being performed, queer clergy are being ordained, churches in Africa and the Philippines are becoming reconciling, and the decision to continue our institutionalized harm against LGBTQ+ people has been rejected or condemned in many areas. The

Church is rejecting its own decision and is in the midst of redefining who we are.

Meanwhile, I've spent my time traveling or communicating with United Methodists in Arizona, California, south Georgia, Illinois, Kansas, Maryland, Minnesota, Montana, upstate New York, Oregon, Pennsylvania, Tennessee, Texas, and rural Wisconsin as well as with folks from various places in Africa, Germany, Norway, and many others around the globe. My hope is that we use this moment to truly reclaim what it means to be *church*—to reclaim the word itself around the world. I want to see us work together toward a global transformation and revolution so that we break the chains of this historical trauma and free ourselves to the powerful possibilities of being overtly political and deeply familial Christ-following assemblies in our world today.

The United Methodist Church is unique in that it's governed by a global body. This has given us many challenges, especially since some of the countries where we exist still outlaw same-sex acts or same-gender marriages. But this also means that there is a potential for safe spaces around the world to be created for LGBTQ+ folks, immigrants, and people of color. This global connection has the potential to be a cooperative vessel of justice for all. As one of my good friends constantly says, "Queer babies will continue to be born around the world whether they like it or not." The struggle for inclusion is an intersectional and global one that involves people who live as LGBTQ+

folks and as people of color, as women, as disabled, as immigrants. It's a global and intersectional challenge to be a Church where all people are not only welcomed but celebrated and affirmed for who God has created them to be. It's a challenge *and* an opportunity.

As the structure of my Church crumbles, and as its discrimination against LGBTQ+ people is broadcast around the world, the Church's eyes have been consequentially opened or reopened to other sins as well. As coalitions and caucuses meet to plan for a new and inclusive future, we've been given the ability to address not only the Church's discrimination against queer people but also its continuing harm against people of color, Native peoples, women, and immigrants. In this moment of great upheaval and revolution, we have the opportunity to be intersectional in our pursuits of justice. That means addressing not only LGBTQ+ exclusion but also the twofold oppression of people of color who identify as queer or as disabled or as transgendered. It's our time to invite the people who have always been on the margins and pushed aside by the Church to be the center of the conversations—to be the dreamers and co-builders of the new Church. It's our time to claim this sacred space and reclaim this idea together.

Whether you attend a Methodist, Presbyterian, Catholic, or congregational church, or none at all, this is a unique moment in time for us all. If we look at the Church's history, we see that every five hundred years the Church goes through a massive re-creation, a change in its structure and identity. In 1054, the East and the West divided in what is called "the Great Schism." The Church split and the Eastern Orthodox Church emerged as separate from the Roman Catholic Church. In 1517, Martin Luther nailed his Ninety-Five Theses to the church doors in Germany and the Protestant Reformation began. It's 2019. We're at our five-hundred-year mark. It's our turn in history to transform the Church and reclaim our assemblies as political in nature and transformational in practice. It's time we separate ourselves from the empire again and align ourselves once more with the underpaid, the unhoused, the previously rejected and condemned. It's our time in history to reclaim what it means to be the Church.

You might be thinking, "How could we possibly do that?" or "Why should we care about this old institution?" You know as well as I do that we live in a time where it's cool to be spiritual but hard to be Christian—and for good reason. The Church has institutionalized racism, sexism, and homophobia, and many folks in our generation don't want anything to do with it. We've said "no more" to the discrimination, and in many places that means "no more" to the Church as well. But I believe that the deep desire in all of us to be loved and to love will always need a place where it can be nurtured, and we can make the Church that place for all of us. We can separate the meaning of church from its discriminatory practices, and we can create something liberating.

The problem isn't the idea of church itself; the problem is with the way it has been harmfully done for so long. It's our turn to take up the baton and continue this marathon toward the promised land of inclusion—a marathon that our ancestors have been running for decades. Each of us can change the identity of these assemblies called church and change the experiences of folks who call them home. You have a voice. We have the chance to pass a rainbow chalice or a hug of appreciation as part of the religious revolution. We've got the tools to start this process, and it's time we get to work.

You're ready to help others chisel away at the harmful statues of God that weigh heavily upon us. You've got the tools to carefully share your experiences and your understanding of what the Bible says and doesn't say. You've been given the opportunity to take off the costume you might still be wearing and embrace the beautifully created you that you are. It's time for us young queer kids, black and brown kids, and kids at the intersections of so many oppressed identities to bring on the revolution. God can do amazing things when God's people are listening and willing to rise up against the status quo. Even if you're not speaking at a microphone in front of thousands of people, your story has the power to impact someone. And if we each impact someone, together we're making a world of difference.

So, here's to us, the generation of queer kids and brown kids and immigrant kids and brown trans immigrant kids who are differently abled and passionate about creating a better world. Here's to our willingness to take the baton from those who have worked so hard to get us where we are, or to run alongside those older folks who are able to continue the race with us. May we remember their sacrifices and move forward, bending the moral arc of history that much further toward justice for all. We are the Church, and it's time for us to reclaim what it means to be Church—together.

NOTE

1. Donald J. Trump, retweet from Wayne Allyn Root, ". . . like he's the King of Israel. They love him like he is the second coming of God," Twitter, August 21, 2019, https://twitter.com/realDonaldTrump/status/1164138796205654016.

ACKNOWLEDGMENTS

This book feels like the binding together of so many meaningful moments throughout my life this far. To bring these pages together in an (hopefully) engaging way took more than long hours staring at a computer screen in airports around the US. Each church, each human being who shared their story with me, and each mentor I've had along the way has been part of this process—the process of finding my voice. I especially want to thank my family, whose openness and willingness to learn saved me from the fate of so many other LGBTQ+ kids. To Rachel and Brooke, your continued friendship, and "welcome back to campus" gathering in our college dorm after my speech, held me in a loving community when I most needed it. I'd also like to thank the deans, faculty, staff, and my fellow students at Boston University School of Theology, whose support and spiritual direction have already begun to impact me profoundly. I am also extremely thankful for my partner, Richard Lopp, whose patience, love, and support have grounded me while our lives changed overnight with this new celebrity.

ACKNOWLEDGMENTS

I must also thank the woman who guided, curated, and crafted the book that has made it into your hands, Maria Mayo. Maria is not only a fabulous editor; she has become a dear friend and "my person." I'd also like to thank the staff of Abingdon Press, especially Susan Salley, and Brian Milford of The United Methodist Publishing House (UMPH). Their support and invitation to write is a gift that not many twenty-two-year-olds receive. Because I am currently Abingdon's youngest author, new and brilliant ways of thinking and interacting took place. I'll never know the extent of your creativity and adaptive work, but know that I am grateful. I'm thankful for their willingness to embrace younger generations as we seek to make this world a better place together.

And finally, thank you. By reading this book you've entered into a difficult but hopefully life-giving journey. You, or the young queer people you interact with, will hopefully find ways to reconcile your faith and the gift that is your sexuality. It's an act of courage for queer folks to step into religious spaces—or to read religious material. Thank you for your courage.